UNBELIVABLE INTERESTING HISTORY STORIES FOR CURIOUS MINDS

BRIAN LAWSON

COPYRIGHT

TABLE OF CONTENTS

INTRODUCTION

Welcome to "Unbelievable Interesting History Stories for the Curious Minds"! History isn't just about dates and old events. It's like a thrilling journey through time, full of amazing stories about how people lived, made discoveries, and experienced events that changed the world. Picture yourself wandering through ancient cities, witnessing grand battles, or finding lost treasures—all these exciting moments are part of our history.

In this book, we'll dive into some of the most astonishing stories from the past. We'll explore tales of brave heroes, mysterious discoveries, and events so surprising they almost seem made up. Each story is a fascinating adventure, showing how the past continues to spark our imagination and inspire us today.

So, get ready to uncover the secrets of history and see how amazing our world's past can be. Let's embark on this adventure together and discover the incredible stories that make history truly extraordinary.

Some history stories stand out because they defy our expectations. They aren't just ordinary events; they involve daring actions, unexpected finds, and mysterious people whose lives were full of excitement. These stories make us wonder, "How did that happen?" and "What made these moments so special?"

Think about a bold explorer finding a hidden city or a scientist discovering something amazing by chance. These are the kinds of stories that captivate us and make us marvel at the incredible things that have happened in the past.

In the chapters that follow, we'll explore these amazing stories. We'll reveal the secrets behind these extraordinary events and learn about the fascinating people who experienced them. Get ready to see history in a way that will surprise and inspire you.

CHAPTER 1

THE ENIGMATIC El DORADO: THE CITY OF GOLD

Imagine a city so dazzling that it was said to be covered in gold, its streets and buildings gleaming with the precious metal. This city was known as El Dorado, a name that means "The Golden One." For centuries, explorers and treasure hunters dreamed of finding this legendary place, but it seemed to vanish like a mirage.

The story of El Dorado began in the early 16th century, when Spanish explorers arrived in South America. They heard tales from the indigenous people about a king who covered himself in gold dust and then washed it off in a sacred lake. This king, and the city he ruled, was said to be overflowing with gold. The Spanish were captivated by these stories and believed that finding El Dorado would make them incredibly rich.

The search for El Dorado turned into a quest that took many lives and consumed countless resources. One of the first explorers to search for El Dorado was Gonzalo Pizarro. In 1532, Pizarro set off with a group of men on an expedition deep into the South American jungle. They faced immense challenges, including harsh weather, disease, and attacks from indigenous tribes. Despite these obstacles, Pizarro and his team pressed on, driven by the hope of discovering the legendary city.

As they journeyed further into the jungle, Pizarro's men grew increasingly weary. They struggled with dwindling supplies and hostile terrain. Their search led them through treacherous swamps and dense forests, and they had to build makeshift rafts to cross rivers. The dream of finding El Dorado seemed to grow fainter with each passing day.

Eventually, Pizarro's expedition came to an end when the group was forced to turn back due to exhaustion and lack of resources. They returned to Spain with tales of their hardships but no sign of the golden city they had been seeking. The legend of El Dorado continued to captivate the imagination of explorers for years to come, inspiring many others to embark on their own searches.

Despite numerous expeditions, no one ever found El Dorado. Some historians believe that the city of gold was never a real place but rather a mythical construct fueled by the

greed and dreams of those who sought it.
Others think that the stories might have been
based on real cities that were later
embellished with the lure of gold.

El Dorado remains one of history's greatest
legends—a tantalizing mystery that
symbolizes the age-old human quest for
wealth and glory. Its story reminds us of the
power of myth and the lengths to which
people will go in pursuit of their dreams.

CHAPTER2

LOST TREASURE OF THE SPANISH GALLEON

Imagine a ship so laden with treasure that it was said to be overflowing with gold, silver, and precious jewels. This was the Spanish galleon, a majestic vessel that carried immense wealth across the oceans. However, this treasure-filled ship would become famous not for its riches but for its disappearance and the mystery that followed.

The Spanish galleon, known as the "Nuestra Señora de Atocha," was a part of Spain's treasure fleet that sailed between the Americas and Spain. In the late 17th century, these ships were loaded with gold and silver mined from the New World, along with precious gemstones and other valuable cargo. The wealth was meant to fund Spain's empire and its numerous wars.

In September 1622, the Atocha set sail from the port of Havana in Cuba, heading back to Spain. The galleon was part of a convoy that included several other treasure-laden ships. However, a fierce hurricane struck the fleet as it made its way across the treacherous waters of the Florida Keys. The storm was so powerful that it scattered the ships and sent them crashing into the reefs and shoals.

The Atocha was among the vessels that were lost to the storm. It sank off the coast of the Florida Keys, taking with it a staggering amount of treasure. The ship's crew and passengers were lost, and the precious cargo was submerged in the deep ocean, never to be seen again—or so it was thought.

For centuries, the story of the Atocha's treasure was little more than a legend. The exact location of the shipwreck remained unknown, and many treasure hunters who attempted to find it met with failure. The legend of the Atocha's lost treasure inspired

numerous expeditions, but none succeeded
in recovering the riches from the deep sea.

The mystery of the Atocha's treasure
remained unsolved until the 1980s when a
determined treasure hunter named Mel
Fisher embarked on a new quest. Fisher,
driven by the allure of the lost treasure,
spent years searching the waters off the
Florida Keys. He faced numerous setbacks,
including financial difficulties and legal
battles, but his perseverance never wavered.

In 1985, Fisher's team finally made a
breakthrough. After years of searching, they
discovered the wreck of the Atocha lying in
the sandy seabed. The shipwreck was found
in relatively shallow waters, which made the
recovery of its treasure possible. Fisher and
his team embarked on an extensive
excavation, uncovering a fortune in gold
coins, silver bars, and priceless gemstones.

The discovery of the Atocha's treasure was a
momentous event, as it revealed an

incredible haul of riches that had been lost for over 350 years. The find included gold doubloons, silver ingots, and emeralds of breathtaking quality. The recovery of the treasure also shed light on the tragic fate of the ship and its crew, who had perished in the storm.

Today, the story of the Atocha's treasure is celebrated as one of the greatest maritime discoveries of the 20th century. The recovered artifacts are displayed in museums, offering a glimpse into the opulence of the Spanish treasure fleet and the perilous journey it undertook. The saga of the Atocha serves as a testament to the enduring fascination with lost treasures and the relentless pursuit of adventure.

CHAPTER 3

THE MYSTERIOUS CASE OF THE AMBER ROOM

Imagine walking into a palace where the walls are made of glowing, golden amber. It sounds like a magical place from a storybook, doesn't it? Well, once upon a time, such a place really existed. This enchanting room was called the Amber Room, and it was one of the most stunning creations of the 18th century.

The Amber Room was located in the Catherine Palace, just outside St. Petersburg, Russia. Its walls were covered in panels of amber, shimmering in shades of gold and honey. Intricate patterns were made from mirrors and gemstones, creating an effect that made the room look like it was bathed in sunlight, even on the darkest of days. People who saw it called it the "Eighth Wonder of the World" because it was so extraordinary.

But during the chaos of World War II, something dreadful happened. As the war reached Russia, soldiers from the invading army came across the Catherine Palace. In the midst of the destruction, the Amber Room disappeared. One day it was there, and the next, it was gone. The room's priceless amber panels, intricate designs, and precious decorations vanished into thin air.

For decades, the Amber Room's disappearance has puzzled and intrigued people from all over the world. Treasure hunters and historians have scoured the ruins of the palace and combed through old records in search of clues. Some think the room was hidden or destroyed during the war, while others believe it was smuggled away and is hidden somewhere still waiting to be found.

Over the years, the Amber Room's mystery has only grown. In a remarkable attempt to capture its lost glory, artists and craftsmen have painstakingly recreated parts of the room using the same techniques and materials. These recreations give us a glimpse of its former beauty but leave the original Amber Room's secrets still waiting to be uncovered. The search for this lost treasure is a thrilling adventure, a dazzling puzzle that invites us to explore the hidden corners of history.

CHAPTER4

HUNT FOR CLEOPATRA 's LOST TOMB

Now let's journey back to ancient Egypt, where another thrilling treasure hunt is taking place. Cleopatra, the famous queen who ruled Egypt over 2,000 years ago, was known for her intelligence and charm. She captivated the rulers of Rome and led Egypt with great skill. But after her dramatic death, her final resting place became one of history's greatest mysteries.

Cleopatra's tomb is believed to be hidden somewhere in Egypt, but no one knows its exact location. Ancient records and legends suggest it could be buried under the Nile River or hidden deep within the sands of the desert. Despite numerous attempts to find it, Cleopatra's final resting place remains a tantalizing secret.

Modern-day archaeologists and explorers are determined to solve this ancient riddle.

They use cutting-edge technology like ground-penetrating radar and satellite imagery to search for clues. They dig through ancient ruins and analyze old texts to piece together hints about where Cleopatra might be buried. Each discovery brings new hope, but the tomb still eludes their grasp.

Finding Cleopatra's tomb would be like discovering a treasure chest full of ancient secrets. It would not only reveal the final resting place of one of history's most famous figures but also shed light on the grandeur of ancient Egypt. The hunt for Cleopatra's tomb is a fascinating journey into the past, filled with excitement and the promise of incredible discoveries.

As you delve into these stories of lost treasures and hidden riches, imagine yourself as a detective uncovering the secrets of the Amber Room and Cleopatra's tomb. These stories remind us that history is full of wonder and mystery, waiting to be explored and understood.

CHAPTER 5

ASTONISHING FIGURES AND THEIR SECRETS

THE ENIGMATIC LIFE OF NIKOLA TESLA

Imagine a man whose ideas seemed so far ahead of his time that they appeared to come from a different world. That was Nikola Tesla, a genius born in 1856 in what is now Croatia. Tesla was more than just an inventor; he was a visionary whose imagination painted pictures of a future filled with incredible technology and possibilities.

Tesla's most famous invention is the alternating current (AC) system, which transformed how we use electricity. Before Tesla's AC system, electricity could only travel short distances using direct current (DC). But Tesla's breakthrough made it possible for electricity to travel across cities and countries, lighting up homes and powering machines far from the source. Imagine being able to turn on a light or power a device no matter where you are—Tesla's invention made that possible.

But Tesla's brilliance didn't end with AC electricity. He dreamt of ideas that seemed almost magical. He imagined a world where people could send information and power through the air without needing wires. Think of it like the wireless technology we use today, but Tesla envisioned it long before it became a reality. He even experimented with a concept he called the "World Wireless System," which aimed to connect the globe through invisible waves, sharing knowledge and energy across vast distances.Despite his remarkable achievements, Tesla's life was filled with unusual and sometimes troubling experiences. He was known for his eccentric habits, like his intense obsession with pigeons, which he cared for deeply. Tesla also claimed to have received messages from extraterrestrial beings, adding another layer of mystery to his already enigmatic personality.

Financial struggles and fierce competition often hindered Tesla's progress. He faced numerous obstacles, including disputes with other inventors and financial backers who didn't always appreciate his revolutionary ideas. Despite these challenges, Tesla continued to push the boundaries of what was possible, driven by a passion for discovery and invention.

Today, Nikola Tesla is celebrated as a pioneer whose ideas laid the groundwork for much of the modern technology we use. His legacy lives on in the devices and systems that power our world, and his imaginative spirit continues to inspire. Tesla's life was a blend of groundbreaking achievements and fascinating eccentricities, making him one of the most intriguing figures in history. His story reminds us of the incredible possibilities that come from thinking differently and dreaming big.

THE STRANGE ADVENTURES OF ELIZABETH I

Step into the splendid world of Elizabeth I, one of England's most legendary queens. Born in 1533, Elizabeth was the daughter of the formidable King Henry VIII and his second wife, Anne Boleyn. Her birth was the beginning of a dramatic saga that would unfold across her lifetime. Elizabeth's reign, known as the Elizabethan Era, is often celebrated for its profound impact on English history, marked by political upheavals, cultural achievements, and bold adventures.

Elizabeth's life was anything but ordinary. Ascending to the throne in 1558, she inherited a kingdom in turmoil. The religious landscape of England was divided, and her rule was immediately challenged by internal strife and external threats. The political climate was filled with plots and conspiracies, with factions constantly scheming to undermine her authority. Elizabeth had to navigate a complex web of alliances and rivalries, making every decision a high-stakes maneuver.

One of the most remarkable aspects of Elizabeth's reign was her extraordinary political acumen. She was known for her shrewd and strategic mind, using diplomacy and charm to outwit her opponents. Her ability to balance power and manage relationships with other countries was exceptional. Elizabeth's reign was marked by her deft handling of both domestic and international politics. She used her intellect and persuasive skills to maintain stability in a kingdom fraught with conflict.

Elizabeth's personal life was a source of endless fascination and intrigue. She never married, earning her the title of "The Virgin Queen." This decision was both a personal choice and a political strategy. By remaining single, Elizabeth avoided the complications and power struggles that often accompanied royal marriages. It allowed her to retain control over her kingdom and maintain her independence. Her suitors and potential matches were the subject of much speculation, but Elizabeth remained resolute in her choice to rule alone.

Under Elizabeth's rule, England experienced a golden age of cultural and artistic flourishing. This period saw the rise of some of the greatest playwrights and poets in English history. William Shakespeare, whose plays and sonnets captivated audiences, wrote many of his works during Elizabeth's reign. The queen was a patron of the arts, supporting and encouraging creative talents. Her court became a center of cultural activity, reflecting the vibrancy and innovation of the era.

Exploration also thrived during Elizabeth's reign. Adventurous explorers like Sir Francis Drake embarked on daring voyages, expanding England's influence across the globe. Drake's circumnavigation of the world and other expeditions showcased the expanding reach of Elizabeth's England. These explorations not only brought wealth and new territories but also strengthened England's position on the world stage.

Elizabeth I's reign was a rich and intricate blend of political maneuvering, personal strength, and cultural flourishing.Her life was filled with remarkable adventures, from navigating the treacherous waters of court politics to championing the arts and exploration. Her complex relationships with courtiers and her role in shaping England's history make her a compelling and enduring figure. Elizabeth I remains a symbol of leadership, resilience, and the extraordinary potential of one remarkable queen.

CHAPTER 6

EPIC BATTLES AND LEGENDARY HEROES

THE BATTLE THAT CHANGED THE WORLD : THE SIEGE OF TROY

Imagine a city surrounded by towering, impregnable walls, its people brimming with pride and confidence. This was Troy, an ancient city in what is now Turkey, a place of legendary significance. The Siege of Troy, one of the most renowned battles in ancient history, unfolded like a grand epic, with heroism, intrigue, and dramatic twists that have captivated imaginations for centuries.

The story began with a beautiful queen named Helen, who was married to Menelaus, the king of Sparta. Helen's abduction by Paris, a prince of Troy, sparked a fierce conflict between the Greeks and the Trojans. Menelaus, furious over the loss of his wife, rallied the Greek states, calling upon their greatest warriors to wage war against Troy.

The Greeks, led by heroes such as Achilles, a nearly invincible warrior with a legendary temper, and Odysseus, known for his cunning and intelligence, laid siege to the city of Troy. For ten long years, the Greeks struggled to breach the towering walls that protected Troy. The Trojans, led by their valiant prince Hector, defended their city with unwavering resolve. The siege was a time of intense and grueling warfare, filled with bloody battles and heroic deeds on both sides.

The struggle seemed endless, and the Greeks grew desperate. In a brilliant display of strategy, Odysseus conceived one of the most famous deceptions in military history: the Trojan Horse. The Greeks built a colossal wooden horse, hollowed out and big enough to hide a group of their finest soldiers. They left the horse at the gates of Troy as a supposed gift and retreated from the battlefield, pretending to abandon the siege.

The Trojans, believing the Greeks had finally given up, were overjoyed and brought the horse inside their city walls. They celebrated their apparent victory, throwing a grand feast and enjoying the supposed end of the conflict. But as night fell, their celebrations turned to horror.

While the Trojans slept, the Greek soldiers hidden inside the wooden horse quietly emerged. They opened the gates of Troy to their comrades, who had secretly returned under the cover of darkness. The Greek army, now inside the city, launched a surprise attack. Caught off guard and unable to defend themselves, the Trojans were overwhelmed. The Greeks stormed through the city, fighting their way to victory and ultimately capturing Troy.

The fall of Troy marked the end of a long and arduous conflict. The story of the Trojan Horse has become a symbol of cleverness and ingenuity, illustrating how cunning can turn the tide of battle. The Siege of Troy has been immortalized in literature, including the epic poems of Homer, such as the "Iliad" and the "Odyssey," which detail the heroic and tragic events of the war.

This legendary battle, with its dramatic twists and unforgettable heroes, reminds us of the timeless nature of courage, strategy, and human perseverance. The tale of Troy, with its grand deceptions and heroic struggles, continues to be one of history's most fascinating and enduring stories.

THE DARING ESCAPE OF HARRIET TUBMAN

Let's journey into a different kind of heroism, one brimming with courage and determination. Harriet Tubman was a remarkable woman whose bravery and commitment to freedom made her a legend. Born into slavery in the early 1820s, Tubman's life began under harsh and unjust conditions. Despite the cruelty and difficulties of slavery, she was resolute in her desire for freedom.

In 1849, Harriet Tubman made a bold and dangerous decision. After years of suffering, she escaped from her own enslaver and fled to the North, where slavery was abolished. But instead of remaining safe in her newfound freedom, Tubman chose to return to the South repeatedly, driven by a powerful sense of mission. Her goal was to help other enslaved people escape to freedom.

Tubman's journey was fraught with danger and challenges. She became a key conductor on the Underground Railroad, a secret network of safe houses and hidden routes designed to assist enslaved people escaping to freedom. The Underground Railroad was not a literal railroad but a system of people and places committed to helping those in need. Tubman, with her exceptional knowledge of routes and her ability to navigate through treacherous terrain, played a crucial role in this covert operation.

Her trips were often undertaken under the cover of darkness, as escaping slaves had to avoid detection from those who would return them to their enslavers. Tubman's skill in guiding people through dense forests, across rivers, and over dangerous terrain was extraordinary. She employed clever tactics to evade capture, such as using disguises and creating diversions. Her bravery and resourcefulness were instrumental in ensuring the safety of those she helped.

Throughout her time working with the Underground Railroad, Harriet Tubman led over 300 people to freedom. Her daring rescues, combined with her incredible courage and determination, made her a living symbol of the struggle for freedom. She never lost a passenger, a testament to her meticulous planning and fearless leadership.

But Tubman's contributions did not end with her work on the Underground Railroad. During the Civil War, she continued to fight for justice and freedom in new ways. Tubman served as a spy, gathering valuable intelligence for the Union Army. She also worked as a nurse, caring for wounded soldiers and supporting the war effort. Her role in the war further demonstrated her unyielding commitment to the cause of freedom and equality.

Harriet Tubman's story is one of unrelenting courage and selflessness. Her willingness to risk her own life for the freedom of others made her a beacon of hope and a powerful symbol of resilience. Tubman's actions not only changed the lives of those she helped but also inspired countless others to continue the fight for justice and equality. Her legacy endures as a shining example of how one person's bravery can have a profound impact on the world.

CHAPTER 7

INVENTIONS AND DISCOVERIES BEYOND IMAGINATION

THE STORY BEHIND THE INVENTION OF THE INTERNET

Imagine a world where you can instantly connect with anyone, anywhere, at any time. You can share ideas, pictures, and messages with people across the globe in seconds. This incredible ability is possible thanks to the invention of the Internet. The story of how this amazing technology came to be is a journey of creativity and determination.

The Internet, as we know it today, wasn't built overnight. It began in the 1960s with a project called ARPANET. This was a network created by the U.S. Department of Defense to allow different computers to communicate with each other. The goal was to share information quickly and efficiently, especially in case of emergencies. The first message sent over ARPANET was a simple "LO," which was meant to be "LOGIN," but the system crashed after only two letters. Despite this small setback, the project grew and evolved.

In the 1970s, two computer scientists, Vint Cerf and Robert Kahn, made a significant breakthrough. They developed a set of rules called TCP/IP, which allowed different networks to connect and communicate with each other. This was a crucial step in creating the Internet. It was like building a universal language that all computers could understand, regardless of where they were or what kind of machine they were.

As the 1980s rolled around, the Internet continued to expand. In 1989, Tim Berners-Lee, a scientist from Switzerland, introduced the World Wide Web. This was an innovative way to organize and access information on the Internet using hyperlinks, which allowed people to click from one webpage to another. His invention made it much easier for people to navigate and use the Internet.

Over time, the Internet grew from a small project used by scientists and researchers to a global network that connects billions of people. It has transformed how we communicate, learn, and entertain ourselves. The Internet's invention was a remarkable achievement that has changed our world in ways that the early pioneers could hardly have imagined.

THE UNEXPECTED DISCOVERIES OF MARIE CURIE

Now, let's turn to a different kind of discovery, one that changed our understanding of science and the world around us. Marie Curie was an extraordinary scientist whose work with radioactivity opened up new frontiers in science and medicine.

Marie Curie was born in 1867 in Poland and moved to Paris to study at the Sorbonne, where she would later meet her future husband, Pierre Curie. Together, they embarked on groundbreaking research into radioactivity, a term Marie Curie herself coined. Their work focused on understanding mysterious rays emitted by certain elements.

One of Marie Curie's most famous discoveries was the element radium. She and Pierre isolated this element from uranium ore, and they found that radium emitted powerful rays that could kill cancer cells. This discovery was groundbreaking because it opened up new possibilities for treating cancer. The use of radium in medicine began a new era of targeted treatment, helping many people fight this deadly disease.

Marie Curie also discovered another element, polonium, which she named after her homeland, Poland. Her research into these elements revealed that radioactivity was not just a surface property of materials but came from the

atoms themselves. This was a revolutionary idea that changed how scientists understood atomic structure and energy.

Marie Curie's work was not without its risks. At the time, scientists did not fully understand the dangers of radiation exposure. Marie Curie suffered from health problems due to her prolonged exposure to radioactive materials. Despite these dangers, she remained dedicated to her research.

Marie Curie's contributions to science were recognized with two Nobel Prizes, making her the first person to win Nobel Prizes in two different scientific fields: Physics and Chemistry. Her discoveries laid the groundwork for many modern technologies and treatments, and her legacy continues to inspire scientists today.

CHAPTER 8: MYSTERIES OF THE ANCIENT WORLD

THE SECRETS OF THE PYRAMIDS OF GIZA

Imagine standing before a giant stone structure, so massive and ancient that it seems to touch the sky.

These are the Pyramids of Giza, some of the
most famous and mysterious monuments
from the ancient world. Located in Egypt,
these pyramids have stood for thousands of
years, and their secrets have fascinated
people for centuries.

The most famous of these pyramids is the
Great Pyramid of Giza, built for the Pharaoh
Khufu around 2560 B.C. It was the tallest

man-made structure in the world for over 3,800 years. Just think about that: a building that remained the tallest for almost four millennia!

Constructing the Great Pyramid was an extraordinary feat. It is made of millions of huge stone blocks, each weighing several tons. The exact methods used to build these massive structures remain a mystery. Some experts believe that ramps were used to transport the stones to higher levels, while others think that clever machinery might have been involved. Even with modern technology, building such a colossal structure would be a daunting task.

Each pyramid was built as a tomb for a pharaoh, designed to protect the king in the afterlife. Inside the pyramids, there were elaborate burial chambers filled with treasures and items the pharaoh might need in the next world. The walls of these tombs were often decorated with beautiful paintings and inscriptions, providing a glimpse into the lives and beliefs of ancient Egyptians.

What makes the Pyramids of Giza even more fascinating is their alignment. The Great Pyramid is aligned almost perfectly with the four cardinal points of the compass. It's as if the builders had advanced knowledge of astronomy. Some people even speculate that the pyramids were built with celestial alignments in mind, perhaps as part of a grand cosmic plan.

Despite countless studies and explorations, many aspects of the pyramids remain shrouded in mystery. How were the enormous stones cut and transported? How did the ancient Egyptians manage to construct such precise and enduring monuments? These questions continue to intrigue historians and archaeologists, making the Pyramids of Giza one of the greatest puzzles of the ancient

CHAPTER 9

THE LOST CIVILIZATION OF ATLANTIS

Now, let's dive into another great mystery: the lost civilization of Atlantis. Atlantis is a legendary city that many people believe was incredibly advanced and powerful. It was first mentioned by the ancient Greek philosopher Plato around 360 B.C. According to Plato, Atlantis was a magnificent island located beyond the "Pillars of Hercules," which we now know as the Strait of Gibraltar.

Plato described Atlantis as a wealthy and technologically advanced civilization with grand palaces, lush gardens, and powerful machines. The people of Atlantis were said to have built an impressive city with concentric rings of land and water, creating a marvel of architecture and engineering.

But then, something catastrophic happened. According to the legend, Atlantis fell out of favor with the gods. The once-great city was said to have been struck by earthquakes and floods, sinking into the ocean in a single day and night. After its disappearance, Atlantis was lost to history, becoming a symbol of a vanished golden age.

Over the centuries, many people have speculated about the true nature of Atlantis. Some believe it was a real place that was destroyed by a natural disaster, like a volcanic eruption or an earthquake. Others think that Atlantis was purely a myth, created by Plato to illustrate a moral lesson about the rise and fall of civilizations.

Numerous theories have emerged about where Atlantis might have been located. Some suggest that it was in the Mediterranean Sea, while others propose locations as far-flung as the Caribbean or even Antarctica. Despite many explorations and searches, no concrete evidence has been found to prove the existence of Atlantis.

The story of Atlantis continues to captivate imaginations, inspiring countless books, movies, and theories. Whether Atlantis was a real place or just a powerful myth, its story remains a fascinating part of our search for lost civilizations and ancient mysteries. The legend of Atlantis reminds us of the allure of discovering the unknown and the thrill of exploring the mysteries of the past.

CHAPTER 10

EXTRAORDINARY SURVIVAL STORIES

THE INCREDIBLE SURVIVAL OF ERNEST SHACKLETON 's EXPEDITION

Imagine setting out on an adventure to explore one of the most remote and icy places on Earth. This was the challenge faced by Ernest Shackleton and his team in the early 1900s. Shackleton, a British explorer, led an expedition to Antarctica, a place known for its freezing temperatures and treacherous conditions. Their journey, however, would turn into a story of remarkable survival and bravery.

In 1914, Shackleton's goal was to cross the Antarctic continent from one side to the other. He and his crew of 27 men set sail on a ship called the Endurance. They ventured into the icy waters, full of excitement and anticipation. But soon, their adventure took a dangerous turn.

As they approached Antarctica, their ship was trapped by thick sea ice. The Endurance was stuck fast in the frozen sea, and no matter how hard they tried, they couldn't free it. The ice began to press on the ship, and Shackleton knew that they were in grave danger. The crew had to leave their ship behind and make camp on the ice.

The harsh conditions were relentless. Temperatures plummeted, and the men had to live in tents and makeshift shelters. Their food supplies dwindled, and the icy winds made life extremely difficult. Shackleton, however, was determined to keep his men safe. He led them with courage and resourcefulness, making sure that they stayed hopeful and united.

After several months, the ice began to break apart. Shackleton made a brave decision to sail to a nearby island called Elephant Island, using lifeboats to navigate through the treacherous ice-filled waters. This was a remarkable feat, showing Shackleton's skill and leadership.

But their ordeal wasn't over yet. Shackleton and a small group of men set off on a daring journey across the stormy seas in a small lifeboat to get help. They faced massive waves and freezing cold as they sailed to South Georgia Island, where they finally found rescue. They were able to return and save the remaining crew members.

Remarkably, despite the extreme conditions and many challenges, every single member of Shackleton's team survived. Shackleton's leadership and the crew's unwavering spirit turned what could have been a tragedy into one of the greatest survival stories ever told. Their story is a powerful reminder of human

endurance and the strength of the human
spirit.

THE RESILIENT VOYAGES OF THE KON-TIKI

Now let's journey to another incredible survival story—the voyage of the Kon-Tiki. In 1947, a Norwegian explorer named Thor Heyerdahl set out on an adventure across the Pacific Ocean in a balsa wood raft. His goal was to prove a bold idea he had about ancient people and their ability to travel long distances.

Heyerdahl believed that people from South America could have reached Polynesia, a group of islands in the central Pacific, using simple rafts made from balsa wood. To test his theory, he built a raft called the Kon-Tiki, named after an ancient Incan sun god. The raft was made of balsa wood logs, ropes, and other materials used by early sailors.

In April 1947, Heyerdahl and his crew of five set off from Peru, hoping to sail across 4,300 miles of open ocean to Polynesia. The journey was extremely risky. They were traveling on a raft with no modern technology, just the wind and waves guiding them.

The crew faced numerous challenges during their voyage. They encountered storms with fierce winds and giant waves. They also had to deal with the scorching sun and the constant threat of sharks. Their food supplies were limited, and they had to be resourceful to catch fish and find fresh water.

Despite these hardships, Heyerdahl and his crew showed incredible determination and teamwork. They used traditional sailing techniques and navigated using the stars, just as ancient sailors might have done. Their adventure became a test of their survival skills and their belief in their mission.

After 101 days at sea, the Kon-Tiki finally reached the shores of Raroia, a small island in Polynesia. Their successful journey proved that it was possible for ancient peoples to make such long voyages using simple rafts. Heyerdahl's voyage provided valuable insights into how early explorers might have traveled across the vast Pacific Ocean.

The story of the Kon-Tiki is a testament to human courage, ingenuity, and perseverance. Heyerdahl and his crew faced enormous challenges, yet they succeeded in proving their theory and demonstrating the power of exploration. Their journey continues to inspire people to embrace adventure and push the boundaries of what is possible.

THE MYSTERIOUS DISAPPEARANCE OF THE PRINCES IN THE TOWER

Now, let's delve into a gripping historical mystery that has puzzled historians for centuries—the disappearance of the Princes in the Tower. This story begins in 1483, during a turbulent time in English history.

The two princes, Edward V and his younger brother Richard, Duke of York, were the sons of King Edward IV. When Edward IV died, the young Edward V was only 12 years old. His uncle, Richard, Duke of Gloucester, was appointed as the guardian for the young king. However, Richard had his own ambitions and soon declared himself King Richard III.

The two princes were placed in the Tower of London, a grand but grim fortress. They were supposed to be kept safe while their uncle Richard took control of the kingdom. However, after Richard became king, the princes were seen less and less. Rumors began to spread that something terrible had happened to them.

In 1485, Richard III was defeated in battle and killed, but the fate of the two princes remained unknown. Many believed that Richard had ordered their murder to remove any potential rivals to his throne. However, no one knows for sure what happened to the young princes.

Over the years, various theories have been proposed. Some suggest that the princes were murdered by Richard's supporters, while others believe that they may have been killed by Henry VII, Richard's successor, to ensure his own hold on the throne. Some even think that the princes might have been secretly smuggled out of the Tower and lived their lives in hiding.

In 1674, workers repairing the Tower of London found a hidden box containing two skeletons. Many believed these bones might belong to the missing princes. However, after tests and examinations, the exact identity of the skeletons remains uncertain.

The mystery of the Princes in the Tower is one of history's most enduring puzzles. The story of the young princes and their disappearance is a haunting reminder of the intrigue, betrayal, and power struggles that have shaped England's past. Their tale continues to captivate imaginations and inspire countless investigations into one of history's greatest unsolved mysteries.

CHAPTER 12

UNEXPECTED MOMENTS THAT CHANGED HISTORY

THE DAY THE BERLIN WALL FELL

Imagine a wall stretching across a city, dividing people from their families, friends, and freedom. This was the Berlin Wall, a powerful symbol of separation and tension during the Cold War. It was built in 1961, dividing East and West Berlin in Germany. The wall represented the fierce divide between two very different worlds: the communist East and the democratic West.

For years, the Berlin Wall stood tall and imposing, separating families and friends. People living in East Berlin were trapped behind the wall, unable to visit loved ones or experience the freedoms enjoyed by those in West Berlin. The wall became a grim reminder of a divided world and the struggles that came with it.

But then, in 1989, something extraordinary happened. The world was changing rapidly, and the pressure for freedom and unity was growing. On November 9, 1989, a series of events unfolded that would change everything. A mix-up in an official announcement led many East Berliners to believe that the border was open. The news spread quickly, and people rushed to the wall, eager to see if they could finally cross.

As crowds gathered at the Berlin Wall, they were met by surprised border guards who had not been prepared for this sudden wave of people. The mood was electric, and the atmosphere was filled with excitement and hope. People began to climb the wall, celebrating their newfound freedom and the possibility of reunification.

Soon, the wall's barriers were being torn down. The joyful chaos of people breaking through the wall with hammers and picks marked the beginning of a new era. The Berlin Wall came down, symbolizing the end of a painful chapter in history and the beginning of a united Germany. The fall of the Berlin Wall was not just a physical event but a powerful symbol of freedom and change, showing how a single moment can reshape the world.

THE COINCIDENCE THAT ENDED WORLD WAR I

Now, let's dive into an incredible story about an unexpected event that brought a temporary but powerful end to one of the deadliest wars in history—World War I. This story takes place during the early days of the war, in a moment that changed the lives of many soldiers on the front lines.

The First World War was a massive and terrible conflict. Soldiers from many countries were fighting each other in trenches, which were long, narrow ditches dug into the ground. These trenches were filled with mud, water, and the constant threat of enemy fire. The soldiers faced grueling conditions, with little rest and very few comforts. It was a time of great suffering and hardship.

In the midst of this harsh and unrelenting war, a special moment occurred on Christmas Eve in 1914. Even though the war was raging, something extraordinary happened that evening. As night fell and Christmas approached, soldiers from both sides of the conflict found themselves yearning for a break from the relentless fighting.

The night was quiet, and as the cold wind blew across the trenches, something unusual began to happen. Soldiers on both sides started singing Christmas carols. The sound of familiar and comforting songs floated across the battlefield, carried by the wind. It was a magical moment, as the soldiers on one side heard their enemies on the other side joining in.

The carols, such as "Silent Night" and "O Holy Night," created an unexpected atmosphere of peace and camaraderie. As the music filled the air, it was as if the usual noise of war was temporarily drowned out by the spirit of Christmas.

The following morning, on Christmas Day, an extraordinary event took place. Soldiers from both sides of the conflict—British and German troops—cautiously emerged from their trenches. They ventured into No Man's Land, the dangerous and desolate area between the opposing trenches. What happened next was truly remarkable.

In the middle of No Man's Land, soldiers from both sides met. They greeted each other with smiles and friendly gestures, shaking hands and exchanging small gifts like chocolates, cigarettes, and even buttons from their uniforms. The soldiers took time to get to know each other, sharing stories and laughter. Some even organized impromptu soccer matches, playing games together in the middle of the battlefield.

This unexpected Christmas truce was a rare and heartwarming break from the violence. For just a brief time, the soldiers put aside their differences and the harsh realities of war. The truce was not officially planned or sanctioned by their leaders; it was a spontaneous act of goodwill driven by the desire for peace.

Although the truce was short-lived and fighting resumed shortly after, it left a lasting impression on everyone involved. The Christmas truce showed that even in the darkest times, moments of kindness and shared humanity could shine through. It was a powerful reminder that, despite the division and conflict, people could come together in moments of understanding and peace.

The story of the Christmas truce of 1914 remains a poignant example of how a simple act of goodwill can make a profound impact, offering a glimpse of hope and unity amidst the chaos of war.

CHAPTER 13: CURIOUS EVENTS AND UNUSUAL TRADITIONS

THE BIZARRE RITUALS OF ANCIENT CULTURES

Imagine stepping back in time to witness some of the most unusual and fascinating ceremonies from ancient cultures around the world. These rituals, often strange and mysterious to modern eyes, were deeply meaningful to the people who practiced them.

In ancient Egypt, the practice of mummification stands out as one of the most intriguing rituals. Egyptians believed that preserving the body was crucial for the afterlife. To achieve this, they used a complex process that involved removing internal organs, drying the body with natron (a type of salt), and wrapping it in linen bandages. The mummies were then placed in elaborate tombs with treasures and items the deceased might need in the next world. This meticulous process reflected their strong beliefs about life after death and the importance of honoring their gods and ancestors.

Far to the east, in ancient China, the practice of burying alive was once a part of royal rituals. During the Zhou Dynasty, it was believed that the spirits of important people should be accompanied in the afterlife by servants and even animals. This often meant that those who served the deceased in life were buried with them, sometimes alive, to ensure they could continue serving in the next world. This practice, though disturbing to us now, was thought to be an act of devotion and respect.

In the vast lands of the Maya civilization, the ancient Maya performed rituals involving human sacrifice. They believed that offering human blood to the gods was essential for maintaining balance and ensuring the survival of their civilization. These sacrifices were often conducted in grand temples, where priests would make offerings to the gods, believing that this would bring prosperity and protection to their people. This tradition highlights how deeply intertwined their religious beliefs were with their daily lives and governance.

Another striking ritual comes from the Celts of ancient Britain and Ireland. Known for their reverence of nature and the seasons, the Celts celebrated various festivals throughout the year. One of the most notable was Samhain, which marked the end of the harvest season and the beginning of winter. During Samhain, people believed that the boundary between the living and the dead was at its thinnest. They lit bonfires, wore costumes to ward off wandering spirits, and made offerings to ensure protection from supernatural forces. These practices reflected their deep connection to the cycles of nature and the spiritual world.

Each of these ancient rituals reveals something profound about how people in the past viewed their world. From mummification and royal burials to human sacrifices and seasonal festivals, these ceremonies were more than mere practices—they were a way of connecting with the divine, honoring the dead, and

ensuring the well-being of their
communities.

THE PECULIAR HISTORY OF HALLOWEEN

Now, let's unravel the curious history of Halloween, a holiday celebrated with costumes, candy, and spooky decorations. But where did these modern traditions come from? The origins of Halloween are deeply rooted in ancient practices and folklore, evolving over centuries into the celebration we know today.

Halloween's roots can be traced back to an ancient Celtic festival called Samhain, which was celebrated over 2,000 years ago in what is now Ireland, Scotland, and Wales. The Celts believed that on the night of October 31st, the boundary between the living and the dead became blurred. They thought that ghosts of the deceased could return to Earth and cause trouble. To protect themselves, people lit large bonfires and wore costumes to ward off these wandering spirits.

As time passed, the celebration of Samhain began to blend with other traditions. By the 8th century, the Christian church introduced a new holiday called All Hallows' Eve on October 31st, the night before All Saints' Day. This was a time to honor saints and martyrs, and the name eventually shortened to Halloween.

Over the centuries, Halloween became a mix of various customs and influences. In medieval Europe, people would go "souling," which involved going door to door asking for food in exchange for prayers for the deceased. This practice evolved into "trick-or-treating," where children now go door to door asking for candy.

In the United States, Halloween gained popularity in the late 19th and early 20th centuries. Irish and Scottish immigrants brought their traditions with them, and Halloween began to be celebrated with a variety of new customs. Costume parties, haunted houses, and pumpkin carving became popular activities, reflecting a mix of old-world superstitions and modern entertainment.

Pumpkins, which are now synonymous with Halloween, have their own interesting history. Originally, the Celts used turnips to create lanterns that were believed to ward off evil spirits. When Halloween traditions crossed the Atlantic, pumpkins became the preferred choice due to their larger size and easier carving.

Today, Halloween is celebrated with a blend of spooky fun and festive activities. People dress up in costumes, attend parties, and enjoy eerie decorations. The holiday has become a time for creativity, imagination, and playful scares, continuing to evolve while honoring its ancient origins.

CHAPTER 14: EXTRAORDINARY LIVES AND SECRET LEGENDS

THE MYSTERIOUS GENIUS OF LEONARDO DA VINCI

Imagine a person so brilliant that his talents seemed endless—someone who could paint masterpieces, invent incredible machines, and unravel the mysteries of the human body. This was Leonardo da Vinci, a name that has become synonymous with genius and creativity. Born in 1452 in a small town in Italy called Vinci, Leonardo grew up to become one of history's most remarkable figures.

Leonardo's talents were apparent from a young age. He was fascinated by the world around him and had an insatiable curiosity. As a child, he would sketch everything he saw, from the flowers in the fields to the animals in the forests. His drawings were not just pictures—they were detailed observations of nature. This early love of drawing would lay the foundation for his future work as an artist.

Leonardo is best known for his paintings, which are still celebrated today. One of his most famous works is the *Mona Lisa This portrait of a woman with a mysterious smile has captivated viewers for centuries. People have speculated about the identity of the woman and the secret behind her enigmatic expression. Some think she might be a real person, while others believe she represents an ideal of beauty. The Mona Lisa remains one of the most recognized and discussed paintings in the world.

Another of Leonardo's masterpieces is The Last Supper. This painting depicts the moment when Jesus announces that one of his disciples will betray him. Leonardo captured the emotions of each disciple with incredible detail, making the scene come alive. The painting is famous not just for its beauty, but also for the way it tells a powerful story through art.

But Leonardo's talents went far beyond painting. He was also an inventor and scientist. His notebooks, filled with sketches and ideas, reveal a mind brimming with imagination. He designed flying machines, like a helicopter that was centuries ahead of its time. He even sketched plans for a diving suit, showing his interest in exploring underwater. Though many of his inventions were never built in his lifetime, they show how ahead of his time Leonardo was.

Leonardo's fascination with the human body led him to dissect corpses, which was unusual and controversial at the time. He meticulously studied the muscles, bones, and organs, creating detailed drawings that helped him understand how the body worked. These studies were not just scientific; they also informed his art, allowing him to create more lifelike figures.

Despite his many talents, Leonardo's life was not without challenges. He struggled with completing projects and often left them unfinished. He moved frequently and worked for various patrons, sometimes facing difficulties in securing commissions. Yet, his legacy endures, not just because of his completed works, but because of the sheer breadth of his creativity and intellect.

Leonardo da Vinci's life was a testament to the power of curiosity and imagination. His ability to blend art, science, and invention made him a true Renaissance man. His contributions continue to inspire people around the world, proving that a single individual's curiosity and creativity can leave an indelible mark on history.

THE INCREDIBLE ADVENTURES OF AMELIA EARHART

Now, let's soar into the story of Amelia Earhart, a woman whose courage and adventurous spirit made her a legend. Born in 1897 in Kansas, Amelia Earhart was fascinated by aviation from a young age. At a time when flying was still a new and daring endeavor, she dreamed of becoming a pilot and breaking records.

Amelia's journey to becoming an aviator began in the early 1920s, a period when few women were involved in flying. She took her first flight in a small airplane and was instantly hooked. Determined to make her mark in aviation, she took flying lessons and quickly became skilled at handling aircraft.

In 1928, Amelia achieved a major milestone when she became the first woman to fly across the Atlantic Ocean. She did not pilot the plane herself during this flight, but she was a passenger and navigator, and the journey made her famous. The flight demonstrated her bravery and helped pave the way for more women to enter the field of aviation.

Amelia's most famous adventure came in 1932 when she made a solo transatlantic flight. This journey was incredibly challenging and dangerous. She flew from Newfoundland, Canada, to Ireland, facing strong winds, mechanical problems, and fatigue. Despite the difficulties, she completed the flight in record time, becoming the first woman to fly solo across the Atlantic. Her achievement earned her international acclaim and solidified her place as a pioneering aviator.

Amelia's adventures didn't stop there. She continued to set records and push boundaries. In 1935, she became the first person to fly solo from Hawaii to the mainland United States. Her achievements inspired many and proved that women could excel in fields traditionally dominated by men.

However, Amelia's most ambitious adventure was her attempt to circumnavigate the globe in 1937. She embarked on this journey with her navigator, Fred Noonan, in a specially modified Lockheed Electra aircraft. The trip was fraught with challenges, including mechanical issues and difficult weather conditions. Amelia and Fred made several stops along the way, but they faced increasing difficulties as they neared the end of their journey.

On July 2, 1937, Amelia and Fred disappeared over the central Pacific Ocean, near Howland Island. Despite extensive search efforts, no trace of their aircraft was ever found. The disappearance of Amelia Earhart remains one of the greatest mysteries in aviation history.

Amelia Earhart's legacy endures as a symbol of courage and determination. Her daring flights broke barriers and inspired countless people. She showed that with passion and persistence, incredible achievements are possible. Her story continues to captivate and inspire, reminding us of the boundless possibilities that come from chasing our dreams, no matter how high the sky may seem.

Both Leonardo da Vinci and Amelia Earhart lived extraordinary lives, each in their unique way. Leonardo's genius spanned art, science, and invention, while Amelia's bravery and skill made her a trailblazer in aviation. Their stories remind us of the power of imagination, courage, and the endless pursuit of discovery.

CHAPTER 15: HISTORIC SHOWDOWNS AND HEROIC FEATS

THE EPIC CLASH AT THERMOPYLAE

Picture a narrow mountain pass surrounded by towering cliffs, where a small group of warriors made a stand against a vast army. This was the scene at the Battle of Thermopylae in 480 BC, one of history's most famous confrontations. The story of Thermopylae is a tale of bravery, strategy, and the fight for freedom.

The battle took place during the Persian Wars, a time when the Persian Empire, under King Xerxes, was attempting to expand its power into Greece. Xerxes led an enormous army, estimated to be hundreds of thousands strong, and sought to conquer the Greek city-states. The Greeks, however, were determined to resist this invasion.

In this critical moment, a Greek force led by King Leonidas I of Sparta stood in defense of their land. Leonidas was a warrior king known for his fierce bravery and military skill. He commanded just 300 Spartans, along with a few thousand Greek allies, to block the narrow pass of Thermopylae, which was the only route for the Persian army to advance.

The Greek forces chose Thermopylae, which means "Hot Gates" due to its hot springs, because its narrowness limited the effectiveness of the Persian numbers. For three days, Leonidas and his men fought bravely, holding off the much larger Persian army. They used their knowledge of the terrain and their skill in close combat to inflict significant casualties on the invaders.

Despite their fierce resistance, the Greeks were eventually betrayed by a local named Ephialtes. He revealed a secret mountain path that allowed the Persians to outflank the Greek position. Realizing that the battle was lost, Leonidas made a crucial decision. He sent most of his troops to safety, choosing to stay behind with his 300 Spartans and a small group of allies.

On the final day of the battle, the Spartans fought to the last man, showing remarkable courage and determination. Though they were eventually overwhelmed and defeated, their stand at Thermopylae became a symbol of heroic resistance. The sacrifice of Leonidas and his men inspired the Greeks to unite and ultimately triumph over the Persians.

The story of Thermopylae teaches us about the power of courage and the impact of standing firm in the face of overwhelming odds. Even in defeat, the Greeks showed

that bravery and sacrifice could leave a
lasting legacy.

THE REMARKABLE STAND OF THE ALAMO

Now, let's travel to a small mission in Texas, where another heroic stand took place. The Battle of the Alamo, fought in 1836, was a crucial event in the Texas Revolution, a struggle for independence from Mexico.

The Alamo was a mission building in San Antonio, Texas, which had been converted into a fort. During the Texas Revolution, it became a symbol of resistance against Mexican rule. The defenders of the Alamo, led by figures such as James Bowie, William B. Travis, and the famous frontiersman Davy Crockett, were a mix of soldiers, adventurers, and settlers.

The Mexican general, Antonio López de Santa Anna, was determined to crush the Texan rebellion. He gathered a large army and laid siege to the Alamo, surrounding it and cutting off supplies. Despite being vastly outnumbered, the defenders of the Alamo were resolute. They prepared for a fierce battle, knowing that their stand was crucial for the future of Texas.

For 13 days, the Texans held out against the Mexican forces. Inside the Alamo, the defenders worked tirelessly to fortify their position and repel attacks. They faced continuous bombardment and assaults but refused to surrender. The defenders' bravery and determination became legendary as they fought to the end, making every effort to defend their stronghold.

On March 6, 1836, the Mexican army launched a final, overwhelming assault on the Alamo. Despite their fierce resistance, the defenders were eventually overrun. Many of the Texans were killed in the battle, and the Mexican forces gained control of the fort. The defenders' heroic stand, however, became a rallying cry for the Texan forces. "Remember the Alamo!" became a powerful slogan, inspiring many to join the fight for independence.

The battle of the Alamo is remembered as a symbol of bravery and sacrifice. The courage of the defenders, who faced certain death rather than surrender, made a lasting impact on the Texas Revolution. Their story shows how the spirit of resistance and the willingness to stand up for one's beliefs can influence the course of history.

CHAPTER 16: ANCIENT MYSTERIES AND LOST WORLDS

THE ENIGMATIC STONEHENGE: BUILDERS AND PURPOSE

Imagine a place where massive stones stand in a circle, their mysterious presence evoking awe and wonder. This is Stonehenge, a prehistoric monument located on the Salisbury Plain in England. Stonehenge is one of the most famous and enigmatic landmarks in the world, and its origins and purpose have puzzled people for centuries.

Stonehenge consists of large upright stones, some of which weigh up to 25 tons, arranged in a circular formation. These stones are topped with horizontal stones called lintels, creating a series of imposing arches. The structure's sheer size and precision make it a remarkable feat of engineering, especially considering it was built around 4,500 years ago, long before modern technology.

One of the great mysteries of Stonehenge is how these enormous stones were transported and erected. The stones, known as sarsens, were likely brought from a quarry located about 20 miles away. To move them, the builders might have used a combination of wooden sledges, rollers, and possibly even water to float the stones closer to their destination. Once at the site, the stones were shaped and set in place using simple tools and techniques that remain impressive even by today's standards.

The purpose of Stonehenge is equally mysterious. Archaeologists and historians have proposed various theories about why it was built. Some believe it was an ancient astronomical observatory, designed to align with the movements of the sun and moon. During the summer and winter solstices, the sun's rays shine through specific gaps in the stones, suggesting that Stonehenge may have been used to mark these important celestial events.

Others think Stonehenge was a place of worship or a burial site. Recent discoveries of human remains near the monument suggest that it might have been a sacred place where people gathered to honor their dead or perform rituals. The presence of these remains indicates that Stonehenge had a significant spiritual or ceremonial role in the lives of the people who built it.

Adding to the intrigue is the fact that Stonehenge was constructed over several stages, spanning from around 3000 BC to 1600 BC. Each phase of construction involved different techniques and modifications, reflecting the changing beliefs and practices of its builders. This long and complex history adds layers of mystery to an already fascinating site.

Despite extensive research and exploration, many questions about Stonehenge remain unanswered. The monument's true purpose, the exact methods used in its construction, and the full extent of its significance are still subjects of debate and investigation. Stonehenge continues to captivate the imagination of people around the world, standing as a testament to the ingenuity and mystery of ancient civilizations.

THE RISE AND FALL OF THE INCA EMPIRE

Traveling from the cold stone circles of Stonehenge to the vibrant highlands of South America, we encounter another fascinating story: the rise and fall of the Inca Empire. The Incas built one of the largest and most advanced civilizations in the Americas, leaving behind a legacy that still captivates historians and explorers.

The Inca Empire, also known as Tawantinsuyu, thrived from the early 15th century until the Spanish conquest in the 16th century. At its height, the empire stretched over 2,500 miles along the western coast of South America, from modern-day Colombia to Chile. It encompassed a diverse range of landscapes, including mountains, valleys, and deserts, and was home to millions of people.

The Incas were skilled engineers and architects, renowned for their ability to adapt to their environment. They built impressive structures, including the famous city of Machu Picchu, which was constructed high in the Andes Mountains. Machu Picchu remains one of the most remarkable archaeological sites in the world, showcasing the Incas' advanced knowledge of construction and urban planning.

One of the key achievements of the Incas was their extensive network of roads and bridges. This network connected various parts of the empire, allowing for efficient communication and transportation. The roads, which stretched over 18,000 miles, were meticulously constructed to navigate the challenging terrain of the Andes. They included suspension bridges made from woven grass and stone-paved pathways that facilitated trade and military movements.

The Inca society was highly organized and centralized. The emperor, known as the Sapa

Inca, held absolute power and was considered a divine ruler. The Incas had a complex system of government, with officials overseeing various regions and ensuring that resources were distributed effectively. They also developed an extensive record-keeping system using knotted strings called quipus to record information.

Despite their achievements, the Inca Empire faced significant challenges. The arrival of Spanish conquistadors, led by Francisco Pizarro, marked the beginning of the empire's downfall. The Spanish, armed with superior weaponry and aided by indigenous allies who were discontented with Inca rule, launched a series of attacks against the empire. The Inca leader, Atahualpa, was captured and executed, leading to the collapse of Inca resistance.

The Spanish conquest had devastating effects on the Inca civilization. The empire's cities were destroyed, its treasures looted, and its people subjected to harsh colonial rule. The Inca culture and way of life were dramatically altered as Spanish influence spread throughout the region.

Yet, despite the fall of their empire, the legacy of the Incas endures. Their architectural marvels, agricultural innovations, and cultural traditions continue to be studied and admired. The descendants of the Incas, known as Quechua and Aymara peoples, still live in the Andes and preserve many aspects of their ancestral heritage.

The story of the Inca Empire is a testament to the grandeur and complexity of ancient civilizations. From their rise to their ultimate decline, the Incas left an indelible mark on history. Their achievements and struggles provide valuable insights into the power and fragility of great empires, and their legacy continues to inspire awe and fascination.

CHAPTER 17: DARING ESCAPES AND SURVIVAL TRIUMPHS

THE GREAT ESCAPE FROM COLDITZ CASTLE

Picture a massive, medieval fortress surrounded by tall stone walls and thick barbed wire. This was Colditz Castle, a German prison camp during World War II, known for being nearly impossible to escape. Yet, inside this fortress, a group of daring Allied prisoners made an audacious plan to break free, turning Colditz into a legendary site of courage and ingenuity.

Colditz Castle was designed to hold high-ranking prisoners who had managed to escape from other camps. Its formidable structure, combined with intense security measures, made it seem like an unbreakable fortress. The castle, perched on a hilltop in Germany, was surrounded by steep cliffs and a deep moat, creating a nearly insurmountable barrier for anyone trying to get out.

However, the prisoners inside were not easily discouraged. Among them were some of the most resourceful and determined individuals from various Allied nations, including Britain, France, and the Netherlands. Despite the strict surveillance and the watchful eyes of the guards, these prisoners began devising plans to outwit their captors.

One of the most remarkable aspects of their escape attempts was their creativity. The prisoners used their skills and resources to build an array of ingenious devices and tools. They created hidden tunnels, fabricated makeshift clothing, and even constructed a glider in an attempt to fly over the castle walls. Their ingenuity knew no bounds as they continued to test their escape plans in secret.

One notable escape plan involved digging a tunnel that stretched from their living quarters to the outside of the castle walls. The prisoners spent months working on this tunnel, carefully disguising their work and avoiding detection. Despite numerous setbacks and close calls, their persistence paid off. In 1942, several prisoners successfully made it through the tunnel and fled into the surrounding countryside.

Another impressive escape attempt involved creating a false identity and disguising themselves as German soldiers. The prisoners managed to steal uniforms and documents, allowing them to move around the castle and gather crucial information. Using their new disguises, they tried to blend in with the guards and gain access to restricted areas.

Despite their best efforts, not all escape attempts were successful, and many of the escapees were recaptured. However, their bravery and determination became the stuff of legend. The story of Colditz Castle's daring escapes continues to inspire and captivate people around the world, highlighting the extraordinary resilience and ingenuity of those who faced seemingly insurmountable odds.

THE SURVIVAL STORY OF THE ANDES PLANE CRASH

Imagine being stranded in a remote, snow-covered mountain range, with freezing temperatures and no help in sight. This was the terrifying reality faced by the survivors of the Andes plane crash, a dramatic and harrowing tale of survival against all odds.

In October 1972, a Uruguayan Air Force plane, carrying 45 passengers and crew, crashed into the rugged Andes Mountains while en route to Chile. The crash left the survivors stranded high in the mountains, surrounded by treacherous terrain and facing extreme cold. With no immediate way to call for help, their situation quickly became dire.

The survivors, including members of a rugby team and their friends and family, had to confront the harsh realities of their predicament. The wreckage of the plane was severely damaged, leaving them without shelter, adequate food, or proper clothing. The temperature plummeted, and the survivors faced the constant threat of avalanches and frostbite.

In the midst of their desperate struggle for survival, the survivors had to make some incredibly tough decisions. With no food sources available, they made the agonizing choice to use the bodies of those who had died in the crash as a source of nourishment. This grim decision was made with a heavy heart but was crucial for their survival.

As the days turned into weeks, the survivors faced mounting challenges. They had to navigate the harsh mountain environment, finding ways to stay warm and ration their limited supplies. The high altitude and freezing temperatures made every task more difficult, but the group's determination and teamwork kept them going.

After enduring 72 days of extreme hardship, the survivors' hope began to wane. However, a small group of them decided to venture out in search of help. They embarked on a grueling trek through the snow-covered mountains, covering more than 60 miles on foot. Their journey was fraught with danger, but their determination to survive drove them forward.

Finally, after an exhausting and perilous journey, the rescuers were able to locate the remaining survivors and bring them to safety. The dramatic story of their survival made headlines around the world, highlighting their incredible resilience and the human spirit's capacity to endure even the most extreme conditions.

The Andes plane crash survival story remains a powerful testament to human courage and perseverance. It serves as a reminder of the strength and determination that can emerge in the face of overwhelming adversity. The survivors' harrowing experience and their eventual rescue continue to inspire and resonate, offering a profound example of hope and endurance against the odds.

CHAPTER 18: ROYAL SECRETS AND IMPERIAL MYSTERIES

THE HIDDEN CHAMBERS OF KING TUTANKHAMUN

Picture a secret world, buried beneath layers of sand and rock, waiting to be discovered. This was the world of King Tutankhamun, an ancient Egyptian ruler whose tomb was found in 1922 by the brave archaeologist Howard Carter. King Tutankhamun, often called "King Tut," lived over 3,000 years ago, and his tomb would become one of the most famous archaeological finds in history.

King Tutankhamun was just a boy when he became pharaoh, leading ancient Egypt through a time of change. His reign was short, lasting only about ten years, and he died at around 18 or 19 years old. Because he was so young, the treasures placed in his tomb were meant to help him in the afterlife and give him the comforts he enjoyed in life.

The Valley of the Kings, where King Tut's tomb was hidden, is a place where many Egyptian rulers were buried. For centuries, this valley was covered in sand and forgotten. It wasn't until Carter and his team began digging that they stumbled upon the entrance to a tomb unlike any other.

When Carter first peered into the tomb, he found a treasure trove of incredible artifacts. Gold, jewels, and intricate artworks filled the space, untouched for millennia. Among the most stunning discoveries was the famous gold mask of King Tutankhamun. This mask, which covered his mummified face, was made of solid gold and decorated with precious stones. It is now one of the most recognizable symbols of ancient Egypt.

The tomb contained not only valuable items but also everyday objects meant to accompany the king into the afterlife. There were chariots, weapons, and even board games. Everything found in the tomb helped historians understand the beliefs and practices of ancient Egyptians. The decorations on the walls told stories of the gods and the afterlife, offering a glimpse into how the Egyptians saw the world and what they believed would happen after death.

One of the most exciting parts of the
discovery was the hidden chambers within
the tomb. These chambers were filled with
amazing objects that revealed more about
the king's life and the customs of the time.
The careful arrangement and preservation of
these items gave historians and
archaeologists valuable insights into ancient
Egyptian culture.

Despite the wonders found in King
Tutankhamun's tomb, many mysteries still
surround his life and death. Why did he die
so young? What were the exact
circumstances of his death? Some
researchers believe he may have died from
an illness or an accident, while others
suggest he was the victim of a conspiracy.
The lack of concrete evidence has left many
questions unanswered.

The discovery of King Tutankhamun's tomb
was a monumental event in archaeology. It
opened a window into a world that had been

lost for centuries and captured the
imagination of people all over the globe.
The hidden chambers of King
Tutankhamun's tomb continue to inspire
curiosity and wonder, showing us that even
in the ancient past, there are still many
secrets waiting to be uncovered.

THE MYSTERIOUS DEATHS OF THE ROMANOVS

Now, let's delve into a different kind of mystery—the tragic end of the Romanov family, the last royal family of Russia. The Romanovs ruled Russia for over 300 years, but their reign came to a dramatic and tragic end during the Russian Revolution.

Tsar Nicholas II, the last emperor of Russia, and his family faced a turbulent time. The Russian Revolution of 1917 was a period of great change and chaos, with many Russians demanding an end to the monarchy and the old ways of ruling. Nicholas II and his wife, Alexandra, and their five children were taken from their palace and held under house arrest in a house in Ekaterinburg, a city in the Ural Mountains.

The night of July 16-17, 1918, was marked by a shocking event. The Romanov family was executed in the basement of the house where they were being held. The decision to implement them was part of the broader upheaval of the revolution and was intended to prevent any chance of the Romanovs being restored to power.

The execution of the Romanovs was a brutal and sorrowful event. Nicholas II, Alexandra, and their children—Olga, Tatiana, Maria, Anastasia, and Alexei—were all killed. The method of their execution and the secrecy surrounding it created a cloud of mystery that has lingered for many years.

In the aftermath of the execution, rumors spread that some of the Romanov family members might have survived. One of the most famous stories was about Anastasia, the youngest daughter, who was rumored to have escaped and lived under different identities. Various women came forward claiming to be Anastasia, but none could be definitively proven to be the lost princess.

The mystery surrounding the Romanovs was partially solved in the late 1990s when their remains were discovered and identified through DNA testing. The remains were found in a mass grave near Ekaterinburg, confirming that the Romanovs had indeed been killed. However, questions about the exact details of the execution and the identities of those responsible remain unresolved.

The tragic end of the Romanovs marked the end of a powerful dynasty and a major shift in Russian history. Their story is one of power, downfall, and enduring mystery. The family's deaths and the rumors surrounding their fate continue to captivate historians and the public, highlighting the complex and often tragic nature of royal lives.

CHAPTER 19: TRANSFORMATIVE EVENTS AND UNSEEN SHIFTS

THE UNLIKELY START OF THE AMERICAN REVOLUTION

Imagine a world where a group of colonies, spread across a vast land, suddenly decides to break away from a powerful empire. This is the story of how the American Revolution began—a surprising and transformative event that changed the course of history.

In the late 1700s, the American colonies were part of the British Empire, and their people were growing increasingly unhappy with British rule. Tensions had been building for years due to various taxes and laws imposed by the British government. The colonists felt that these rules were unfair, especially since they had no representation in the British Parliament. The phrase "No taxation without representation" became a rallying cry for those who wanted change.

It all started with seemingly small disputes that built up over time. The Stamp Act of 1765, which required colonists to buy and use specially stamped paper for legal documents, newspapers, and other papers, was one such grievance. The Boston Tea Party of 1773 was another key event where American colonists, protesting a tax on tea, dumped an entire shipment of tea into Boston Harbor. These actions were bold statements against British control, but they also set the stage for a bigger conflict.

The revolution officially began in April 1775 with the battles of Lexington and Concord. These skirmishes were the first military engagements between the American colonists and British soldiers. Despite being poorly equipped, the colonists' determination and knowledge of the local terrain gave them an advantage. As the fighting spread, more and more people joined the cause for independence.

The Continental Congress, a gathering of representatives from the colonies, took a daring step by declaring independence from Britain on July 4, 1776. This decision was formalized with the signing of the Declaration of Independence, drafted primarily by Thomas Jefferson. The Declaration boldly stated that the colonies were no longer under British rule and were now free and independent states.

The American Revolution was not just about battles; it was also about ideas. The revolutionaries believed in concepts like liberty, equality, and self-governance. These ideas were new and radical, challenging the traditional notions of monarchy and colonial rule. The revolutionaries faced enormous challenges, including a well-trained British army and a lack of resources. But their spirit and determination, along with support from countries like France, played a crucial role in their eventual victory.

The war ended in 1783 with the Treaty of
Paris, which recognized the independence of
the United States. The American Revolution
was a remarkable event that transformed the
American colonies into a new nation. It set
the stage for the development of democratic
principles and inspired future movements
for freedom and independence around the
world.

THE UNEXPECTED COLLAPSE OF THE SOVIET UNION

Now, let's shift to a different era and explore a dramatic event that reshaped the world stage—the unexpected collapse of the Soviet Union. This event marked the end of one of the most powerful empires of the 20th century and had far-reaching consequences for global politics.

The Soviet Union, officially known as the Union of Soviet Socialist Republics (USSR), was a major global power during the Cold War. It was a superpower with a vast territory stretching from Eastern Europe to Asia and was known for its communist government and rivalry with the United States. The USSR was seen as a formidable force, and its collapse was something few anticipated.

By the 1980s, the Soviet Union was facing serious problems. The economy was struggling due to inefficient planning and excessive government control. The country was also burdened by an arms race with the United States, which drained resources. Internally, there were growing demands for political reform and greater freedom.

A key figure in the story of the Soviet Union's collapse was Mikhail Gorbachev, who became the leader of the USSR in 1985. Gorbachev introduced major changes with his policies of glasnost(openness) and perestroika (restructuring). Glasnost aimed to increase transparency and freedom of expression, while perestroika sought to reform the economy and government. These reforms were intended to modernize the Soviet system but also led to greater demands for change and criticism of the government.

Gorbachev's reforms sparked a wave of political and social movements across the

Soviet Union. People began to speak out more openly about their dissatisfaction with the government and the economic situation. Nationalist movements in various Soviet republics, such as Ukraine, the Baltic states, and Georgia, grew stronger and started pushing for independence.

The situation came to a head in 1989 and 1990. The fall of the Berlin Wall in 1989 symbolized the collapse of communist control in Eastern Europe and inspired similar movements within the Soviet Union. In 1991, the Soviet Union faced a critical moment when a coup attempt by hardline communists aimed to seize control from Gorbachev. The coup failed, but it weakened the central government and accelerated the push for independence among the republics.

By December 1991, the Soviet Union officially dissolved. The leaders of the republics agreed to form the Commonwealth of Independent States (CIS), effectively ending the existence of the Soviet Union.

The collapse was a sudden and surprising turn of events, leaving a profound impact on global politics. It led to the emergence of new independent nations and significantly altered the balance of power in the world.

The end of the Soviet Union marked the conclusion of the Cold War era and ushered in a new period of global relations. It was a dramatic and unforeseen event that reshaped international dynamics and had lasting effects on the political and economic landscape.

CHAPTER 20: QUIRKY CUSTOMS AND HISTORICAL ODDITIES

THE FASCINATING WORLD OF ANCIENT GREEK ORACLES

Picture a time when people turned to mysterious figures for guidance, hoping to glimpse the future through enigmatic prophecies. This was the world of ancient Greek oracles, whose words held great power and influence over many aspects of life.

The most famous oracle of ancient Greece was the Oracle of Delphi. Delphi, nestled on a mountainside, was considered the center of the world by the Greeks. People from all

over came to seek advice from the Pythia,
the priestess who served as the mouthpiece
of Apollo, the god of prophecy. Visitors
would climb the winding path to the temple,
eager for a glimpse of their fate.

Inside the temple, the Pythia would sit over
a fissure in the earth, from which mysterious
vapors were believed to rise. As she inhaled
these vapors, she entered a trance-like state.
In this altered state, her words were often
cryptic and hard to understand. Her
prophecies came in the form of riddles and
verses, and it was up to the visitors to
interpret their meaning.

One famous story involves King Croesus of Lydia. He visited the Oracle of Delphi before launching a military campaign against Persia. The oracle told him, "If you cross the river, a great empire will fall." Croesus interpreted this as a promise of victory over Persia. However, his own empire was defeated, proving the oracle's words to be true in an unexpected way.

Another well-known oracle was the Oracle of Dodona, located in a sacred grove of oak trees. Here, the rustling of the leaves was believed to convey messages from Zeus, the king of the gods. The priests of Dodona would listen to the sounds of the leaves and interpret them as divine advice. These interpretations guided decisions ranging from politics to personal matters.

The Sibyl of Cumae was another legendary figure. This oracle delivered her prophecies in the form of verses written on leaves. According to myth, she had the power to see into the future, but her gift came with a curse. She was granted an extended life by Apollo, but not eternal youth. As she grew older, her prophecies became harder to decipher, adding to the enigma surrounding her.

These oracles were more than just curious figures—they were deeply embedded in the fabric of Greek society. Their prophecies influenced everything from wars to personal choices. Consulting an oracle was considered a way to connect with the divine and gain insight into the unknown.

THE ECCENTRIC PRACTICES OF MEDIEVAL ALCHEMISTS

Now, let's venture into the quirky world of medieval alchemists, whose strange experiments and mystical beliefs were a fascinating blend of science and superstition. Alchemy, a precursor to modern chemistry, was the quest to transform base metals into gold and discover the secret to eternal life.

Medieval alchemists worked in secretive, dimly lit laboratories filled with strange equipment like crucibles, retorts, and alembics. They combined various substances, heated them, and performed mysterious rituals, all in the hope of uncovering hidden secrets. Their writings were filled with cryptic symbols and enigmatic language, making their work seem almost magical.

One of the most famous alchemists was Nicolas Flamel, a French scribe who became legendary for supposedly discovering the Philosopher's Stone. The Philosopher's Stone was believed to be a substance that could turn any metal into gold and grant eternal life. While there is little evidence that Flamel actually achieved this, stories about his discovery contributed to his mystique.

Alchemists were not just interested in turning base metals into gold; they were also fascinated by the idea of spiritual transformation. They believed that through their experiments, they could purify their own souls. This quest for personal and spiritual enlightenment was a significant part of their practice.

Another aspect of alchemy was its connection to astrology. Alchemists believed that the positions of the stars and planets influenced their work. They would carefully time their experiments according to astrological charts, hoping to align their efforts with cosmic forces. This blend of astrology and chemistry added an extra layer of mystery to their practices.

Medieval alchemists also created elaborate, symbolic diagrams called "alchemical symbols." These symbols represented various substances and processes, and they were used to communicate ideas in a way that was both secretive and symbolic. For example, a circle with a cross inside it was often used to represent the Philosopher's Stone.

Despite their eccentric methods, alchemists made significant contributions to the development of modern science. They discovered several chemical processes and substances, including acids and alkalis. Their work laid the groundwork for future discoveries and the establishment of chemistry as a scientific discipline.

Alchemical practices eventually fell out of favor as science progressed and more empirical methods were developed. However, the eccentric world of medieval alchemy remains a captivating chapter in the history of science. The combination of mystical beliefs and early scientific experimentation highlights humanity's enduring curiosity and quest for understanding.

CHAPTER21:RIVETING CONFLICTS AND LEGENDARY BATTLES

THE SIEGE OF CONSTANTINOPLE: A CLASH OF EMPIRES

Imagine a city with high, mighty walls, guarding a wealth of history, art, and power. This was Constantinople, a grand city located where Europe meets Asia, straddling two worlds. The year was 1453, and the city faced one of the most dramatic sieges in history.

Constantinople was the capital of the Byzantine Empire, a powerful realm that had survived for over a thousand years. Its walls were legendary, thick and strong, designed to keep out any attackers. But the mighty Ottoman Empire, led by the ambitious Sultan Mehmed II, was determined to conquer this jewel.

The Ottomans surrounded Constantinople with a massive army. They brought in thousands of soldiers, enormous cannons, and war machines. For months, they besieged the city, cutting off supplies and launching relentless attacks. The Byzantine defenders, under Emperor Constantine XI, fought bravely but were vastly outnumbered. The siege became a battle of endurance and strategy, with the city's defenders using every trick in their book to repel the invaders.

One of the most dramatic moments was the use of massive cannons by the Ottomans. These were some of the largest ever built, capable of hurling enormous stones at the city's walls. The cannons pounded the defenses, creating breaches that allowed the Ottomans to get closer.

In the final days, the Ottomans launched a final, desperate assault. Thousands of soldiers swarmed the city walls. The Byzantines fought fiercely, but the sheer number of attackers began to take its toll. On May 29, 1453, the Ottomans broke through the walls and captured Constantinople.

The fall of Constantinople marked the end of the Byzantine Empire and a significant shift in history. The Ottomans turned the city into their new capital, Istanbul, and their empire continued to grow. This clash of empires changed the course of history and had a lasting impact on the world.

THE LAST ROANOKE COLONY DRIFTING

In another corner of the world, far from the grand walls of Constantinople, a different kind of battle unfolded in 1879. This was at a remote outpost called Rorke's Drift in southern Africa, and it was a fight for survival against overwhelming odds.

The setting was the Anglo-Zulu War, a conflict between the British Empire and the Zulu Kingdom. Rorke's Drift was a small mission station manned by just over a hundred British soldiers. They were stationed there to keep an eye on the Zulu forces and protect British interests in the region.

On January 22, 1879, news reached Rorke's Drift that the British had suffered a massive defeat at the Battle of Isandlwana. Thousands of Zulu warriors had overwhelmed a much larger British force, and now they were advancing toward Rorke's Drift.

The small garrison at Rorke's Drift prepared for what seemed like a certain defeat. The Zulus, known for their fierce fighting skills, were coming in large numbers, estimated at around 4,000 warriors. The defenders, under the command of Lieutenants John Chard and Gonville Bromhead, quickly fortified the outpost, using bags of mealie (corn) to create defensive walls.

As night fell, the Zulus launched their attack. The British soldiers fought back with everything they had. They used rifles, bayonets, and even the walls of the mission station to fend off the attackers. The battle was fierce and chaotic, with the defenders fighting hand-to-hand in the dark.

Throughout the night, the Zulus pressed the attack, but the defenders held their ground. Despite being vastly outnumbered, the

British soldiers managed to repulse wave after wave of assaults. Their bravery, discipline, and determination turned the tide in their favor.

The battle continued until dawn, when the Zulus finally withdrew. The defenders had managed to hold off the overwhelming force, and Rorke's Drift became a symbol of courage and tenacity. Eleven Victoria Crosses, the highest military honor in Britain, were awarded to the defenders for their bravery during the battle.

The stand at Rorke's Drift was more than just a military engagement; it was a testament to the human spirit's resilience. Against overwhelming odds, a small group of soldiers defended their position with remarkable bravery. Their story became legendary, highlighting the clash between two different worlds and the extraordinary feats that can occur in moments of extreme conflict.

CHAPTER 22: HIDDEN TREASURES AND LOST CITIES

THE ENIGMATIC FATE OF THE LOST CITY OF OZ

Imagine a city so beautiful and rich that it seems like a story from a dream. This is what explorers hoped to find when they searched for the Lost City of Z. Hidden somewhere deep in the jungles of South America, this mythical city was thought to be a land of gold and wonder. Its story began with a man named Percy Fawcett, an adventurer with a passion for discovering lost worlds.

Percy Fawcett was a British explorer in the early 20th century. He had already made a name for himself with his explorations in

South America, and he became obsessed with finding this legendary city. According to old tales and mysterious maps, the Lost City of Z was a place of immense wealth and advanced civilization, hidden from the modern world.

In 1920, Fawcett set out on an expedition to find this fabled city. He believed it was somewhere in the vast Amazon rainforest, an area that was almost unknown to outsiders at the time. With a small group of men, he ventured into the dense jungle, navigating through thick foliage, wild animals, and treacherous rivers.

Fawcett's journey was filled with challenges. The jungle was harsh and unforgiving, and they faced many dangers, including diseases and hostile tribes. Despite these obstacles, Fawcett pressed on, driven by the dream of discovering the Lost City of Z. He sent letters to his family, describing the marvels he hoped to find and the difficulties he faced.

But in 1925, after months of silence, Fawcett and his team vanished. No one knows for sure what happened to them. Some think they might have been lost to the jungle, while others believe they met with disaster or were attacked by indigenous groups. Despite numerous attempts by other explorers to find them or uncover their fate, the mystery of Fawcett's disappearance and the Lost City of Z remains unsolved.

The story of the Lost City of Z is one of adventure, mystery, and the enduring human spirit. It captures our imagination, reminding us of the allure of the unknown and the lengths to which people will go to uncover hidden treasures and lost worlds. The legend of the Lost City of Z continues to inspire explorers and dreamers, sparking curiosity about what might still be hidden in the uncharted corners of our planet.

THE SECRET VAULTS OF THE VATICAN

Now, let's turn to another mystery that lies hidden in plain sight—the Secret Vaults of the Vatican. The Vatican, located in Rome, is the spiritual and administrative center of the Roman Catholic Church. But beneath its grand buildings and majestic art lies a hidden world of secrets and treasures.

The Vatican's secret vaults are said to contain some of the most important and mysterious documents and artifacts in the world. These vaults are part of the Vatican Secret Archives, a collection of records and manuscripts that have been kept away from the public eye for centuries. The name "Secret Archives" doesn't mean they're mysterious or illicit; it comes from the Latin word "secretum," which means "private."

The Vatican Archives house documents from as far back as the 8th century, covering a wide range of topics, including historical records, religious decrees, and personal letters from popes. Among these are the official documents from significant events in history, such as the trial of Galileo Galilei, who was tried for his support of heliocentrism, the idea that the Earth orbits the Sun.

One of the most intriguing aspects of the Vatican Archives is the fact that much of it remains closed to the public. Scholars and researchers can access certain parts of the archives, but many documents remain classified. This has led to speculation and curiosity about what secrets the vaults might contain. There are rumors of hidden records about controversial historical figures, ancient religious relics, and even lost knowledge that could change our understanding of history.

The Vatican has been slowly opening up parts of its archives to historians and researchers. In recent years, some documents have been made available to the public, providing new insights into historical events and the workings of the Church. However, the full extent of what is hidden in the Vatican's vaults is still largely unknown.

The Secret Vaults of the Vatican symbolize the mysteries that lie behind the most well-known institutions. They remind us that even in places of great power and history, there are still hidden corners waiting to be explored. The Vatican's archives continue to be a source of fascination and intrigue, offering a glimpse into a world of secrets that connects us to the past in ways we are only beginning to understand.

THE LITTLE-KNOWN LIFE OF HYPATIA OFf ALEXANDRIA

Imagine walking through the bustling streets of ancient Alexandria, a city known for its grand library, bustling markets, and vibrant culture. Amidst this lively setting, one remarkable woman stood out, not for her beauty or wealth, but for her extraordinary intellect and pioneering spirit. This woman was Hypatia of Alexandria, a philosopher, mathematician, and teacher whose story is both inspiring and tragic.

Hypatia was born around 360 CE in Alexandria, a city in Egypt that was a melting pot of Greek, Egyptian, and Roman cultures. Her father, Theon, was a renowned mathematician and astronomer, and he recognized his daughter's exceptional abilities from an early age. At a time when women were rarely seen in academic circles,

Hypatia's talents were extraordinary and rare.

From a young age, Hypatia showed a remarkable aptitude for learning. Her father took her under his wing, teaching her mathematics, astronomy, and philosophy. These subjects were not common for women to study during her time, but Hypatia's brilliance shone through, defying societal norms. Her father's encouragement helped her to thrive in an environment where women's roles were often limited.

As Hypatia grew older, she became a respected teacher and scholar at the Neoplatonic school in Alexandria, a prestigious institution known for its philosophical and scientific teachings. Her lectures attracted students from across the Roman Empire, eager to learn from her innovative ideas and profound knowledge. Hypatia's teachings were grounded in the works of Plato and Aristotle, but she also introduced new perspectives and methods, pushing the boundaries of traditional thinking.

One of Hypatia's most significant contributions was in the field of mathematics. She wrote commentaries on famous mathematical texts, such as those by Diophantus and Apollonius. These works were not just academic exercises; they helped to advance mathematical understanding and influence future generations of scholars. Hypatia's work in astronomy was equally impressive. She is believed to have developed astrolabes, ancient instruments used to measure the position of stars and planets, which were essential for navigation and astronomical studies.

Hypatia's influence extended beyond her scholarly achievements. She was a prominent figure in Alexandria's intellectual and political life. Her wisdom and integrity earned her the respect of many, including political leaders and influential thinkers. Despite the challenges she faced as a woman in a male-dominated society, Hypatia's intellect and character allowed her to navigate these obstacles with grace and success.

However, Hypatia's life was not without its struggles. During her time, Alexandria was a city of deep religious and political divisions. The rise of Christianity and the decline of traditional Greco-Roman philosophies led to increasing tensions. Hypatia, a pagan philosopher, found herself caught in the crossfire of these conflicts. As tensions mounted, her school and intellectual pursuits came under threat.

In 415 CE, Hypatia's life took a tragic turn. A group of Christian extremists, opposed to her teachings and influence, targeted her. Hypatia was brutally murdered by a mob that dragged her from her chariot, attacked her, and killed her in a horrific display of violence. Her death marked a turning point in Alexandria's history and symbolized the decline of classical learning in the face of rising religious intolerance.

Despite the tragic end to her life, Hypatia's legacy endures. Her story serves as a powerful reminder of the importance of intellectual curiosity and the courage to pursue knowledge despite the obstacles. Hypatia's contributions to mathematics, astronomy, and philosophy remain influential, and her life continues to inspire scholars and students around the world.

Hypatia's story also sheds light on the broader historical context of her time. The struggles between different philosophical and religious traditions in Alexandria reflect the complex dynamics of a society in transition. Hypatia's life illustrates the challenges faced by intellectuals in times of cultural upheaval and the sacrifices made in the pursuit of knowledge.

In modern times, Hypatia is remembered not only for her scholarly achievements but also for her role as a trailblazer for women in academia. Her story highlights the potential of individuals to break barriers and make significant contributions to human understanding. Hypatia's life is a testament to the enduring power of intellectual pursuit and the importance of preserving and celebrating the legacy of those who have advanced human knowledge.

CHAPTER 23: HISTORIC DISAPPEARANCES AND UNSOLVED MYSTERIES

THE VANISHING OF THE ROANOKE COLONY

Picture a lush island along the coast of North Carolina in the late 16th century, where a group of settlers from England prepared to start a new life. This island, known as Roanoke, was the site of one of history's most puzzling mysteries—the disappearance of the Roanoke Colony.

The story begins in 1587 when a group of 115 English settlers, including men, women, and children, arrived at Roanoke Island. They were led by John White, a man who had previously explored the area and was now tasked with establishing a permanent colony. The settlers faced many challenges, including harsh weather, unfamiliar terrain, and a strained relationship with local Native American tribes. Despite these difficulties, they managed to set up a settlement and begin their new life.

In August 1587, John White sailed back to England to gather supplies and support for the struggling colony. However, when he arrived, England was embroiled in a war with Spain, and White's return was delayed by several years. By the time he finally returned to Roanoke Island in 1590, he was greeted by an eerie silence. The settlement had vanished without a trace.

White and his men searched the island thoroughly but found no signs of the colonists. All that remained were the abandoned houses and a cryptic clue—a single word carved into a tree: "Croatoan." Croatoan was the name of a nearby island and a Native American tribe living there.

White assumed the colonists had moved to Croatoan Island, but a storm prevented him from investigating further.

Over the years, various theories have been proposed about the fate of the Roanoke colonists. Some suggest they were killed by Native Americans, while others believe they may have assimilated with local tribes. There are even theories that they tried to relocate to a different area but perished along the way. Despite numerous expeditions and investigations, the fate of the Roanoke Colony remains one of history's great mysteries.

THE DISAPPEARANCE OF THE SODDER CHILDREN

Now let's shift to a more recent, but equally chilling mystery—the disappearance of the Sodder children. On Christmas Eve in 1945, the Sodder family's home in Fayetteville, West Virginia, was engulfed in flames. George and Jennie Sodder, along with their four surviving children, managed to escape, but five of their ten children were missing.

The fire was devastating, and although the house was destroyed, no remains of the missing children were ever found. This lack of evidence, combined with a series of strange occurrences, led to a growing belief that the children had been kidnapped rather than perishing in the blaze.

In the months leading up to the fire, the Sodders had experienced several unsettling incidents. They received threatening phone calls and saw a strange man who seemed to be watching their home. The night of the fire, a neighbor reported seeing a strange vehicle parked near the Sodder house, adding to the mystery.

George and Jennie Sodder became convinced that their children were still alive and that the fire was part of a larger plot. They spent the rest of their lives searching for answers. They received various tips and reports over the years, including claims that their children had been seen in different states or even countries. Despite their efforts and a reward of $10,000 for information, no concrete evidence was ever found.

The case took another twist when, in 1949, a letter arrived at the Sodder home containing a photograph of a young man who resembled one of their missing children. The note, which was written in a foreign language, suggested that the boy was one of the Sodder children, but the photograph was never verified.

The Sodders continued their search until their deaths, holding onto the hope that their children might still be out there. The disappearance of the Sodder children remains an open case, with many questions still unanswered. Was it a case of mistaken identity, a kidnapping, or something even more sinister? The true story behind the Sodder children's disappearance remains elusive, leaving a lasting mystery.

CHAPTER 24: FASCINATING TRADITIONS AND QUIRKY PRACTICES

THE ANCIENT RITUALS OF THE SIBERIAN SHAMAN

Imagine a snowy land far in the north, where the cold winds blow and the nights stretch long. In this remote region of Siberia, a world of ancient traditions and mystical practices thrives. The Siberian shaman, a key figure in this world, is a master of rituals that have been passed down through generations.

Siberian shamans are spiritual guides and healers who connect with the spirit world to help their people. Their ceremonies are rich with symbols and practices that are both mysterious and mesmerizing. One of the most intriguing aspects of their rituals is the use of drumming and chanting to enter a trance. When a shaman drums and chants, they believe they are journeying to another realm, where they can speak with spirits and seek their guidance.

During these ceremonies, the shaman wears elaborate costumes and masks. These are not just for show—they represent different spirits and forces of nature. The masks are often carved with intricate designs and painted in vivid colors. Each mask has its own story and purpose, helping the shaman to channel the spirit they are invoking.

Another fascinating element of Siberian shamanism is the use of sacred objects. Shamans carry special tools, like bone rattles and staffs, which are believed to hold powerful spiritual energy. These objects are used in rituals to cleanse spaces, heal individuals, and bring about change. For instance, a rattle might be shaken to drive away bad spirits or to invite positive energy into a home.

One of the most dramatic ceremonies is the "soul retrieval" ritual. In this practice, the shaman helps someone who is suffering from illness or misfortune by calling back lost parts of their soul. The shaman believes that traumatic events or negative experiences can cause parts of the soul to fragment or drift away. By performing the soul retrieval ritual, the shaman aims to restore balance and well-being to the individual.

Siberian shamanism is deeply connected to the natural world. Many rituals honor the spirits of animals, plants, and the earth itself. Shamans often perform ceremonies to thank these spirits for their gifts and to ask for their continued support. This deep respect for nature is a fundamental part of the shamanic tradition, reflecting a harmonious relationship between humans and the environment.

Though shamanism has faced challenges from modernization and external influences, its practices continue to be an important part of Siberian culture. The rituals and beliefs of the Siberian shamans offer a fascinating glimpse into a world where the spiritual and natural realms are intricately connected.

THE ODDITIES OFf MEDIEVAL FESTIVALS

Travel back to medieval Europe, a time of castles, knights, and grand feasts. Medieval festivals were vibrant, lively events filled with customs that might seem strange to us today. These festivals were not just about having fun; they were deeply rooted in the culture and beliefs of the time.

One of the most colorful medieval festivals was the "Feast of Fools." This event, held around the time of the Epiphany, was a chaotic celebration where traditional roles were reversed. For one day, the lowest-ranking members of society could mock and mimic their betters. It was a time of playful disorder, where jesters and common folk took on roles of authority and poked fun at the higher classes. This festival allowed people to express their frustrations and dreams in a way that was both humorous and liberating.

Another curious tradition was the "Tournement of the Mummers." Mummers were actors who performed short, comedic plays in the streets. These plays often involved exaggerated characters and humorous situations, designed to entertain and amuse. The performances were lively and engaging, with plenty of audience participation. The Mummers' plays were a way for people to relax and enjoy themselves, adding a touch of fun to their daily lives.

Medieval festivals also featured elaborate processions, where people dressed in colorful costumes and paraded through the streets. These processions were often part of religious celebrations, such as the "Corpus Christi" festival, which honored the Holy Eucharist. Participants in these processions carried banners, sang hymns, and performed acts of devotion. The parades were a spectacle of pageantry, designed to showcase the community's faith and unity.

One of the most unusual medieval customs was the "Whipping Day." On this day, people would gather to witness a public event where participants were lightly whipped as part of a cleansing ritual. This practice was believed to drive away evil spirits and ensure good fortune for the coming year. Although it may seem strange today, Whipping Day was taken very seriously and was an important part of medieval tradition.

Medieval festivals were also known for their competitive events. One such event was the "Maid Marian Festival," which featured various contests and games. People would compete in archery, wrestling, and other challenges, showcasing their skills and strength. These competitions were not only a source of entertainment but also a way for people to demonstrate their abilities and earn respect.

In addition to these peculiar customs, medieval festivals often included feasting and revelry. Banquets were held with an abundance of food and drink, and the festivities could last for days. Music, dancing, and storytelling were integral parts of the celebrations, providing joy and merriment for all who participated.

FUN FACTS TRIVIA
HISTORY

1. The word "history" comes from the Greek word "historia," meaning "inquiry" or "knowledge acquired by investigation."

2. The Great Wall of China is over 13,000 miles long, making it the longest wall in the world.

3. The Library of Alexandria, one of the ancient world's most famous libraries, once held up to 700,000 scrolls.

4. The Lost City of Z is a legendary city of gold believed to be hidden in the Amazon rainforest.

5. The Vatican Secret Archives are home to documents dating back to the 8th century and are one of the most confidential collections in the world.

6. Hedy Lamarr, a famous actress, co-invented a frequency-hopping technology that laid the foundation for modern wireless communication.

7. Ada Lovelace, often regarded as the first computer programmer, wrote the first algorithm

intended for Charles Babbage's mechanical computer.

8. Leonardo da Vinci designed a flying machine centuries before the Wright brothers achieved controlled flight.

9. Marie Curie was the first woman to win a Nobel Prize and discovered radium and polonium, which were crucial to advancements in radiology.

10. Nikola Tesla's inventions include alternating current (AC) electrical systems and wireless communication technology.

11. The Siege of Constantinople in 1453 marked the end of the Byzantine Empire and the rise of the Ottoman Empire.

12. The Last Stand at Rorke's Drift involved a small British garrison defending against thousands of Zulu warriors in 1879.

13. The Battle of Thermopylae in 480 BCE featured King Leonidas and 300 Spartans making a heroic stand against Persian forces.

14. The Charge of the Light Brigade during the Crimean War was famous for its bravery and disastrous miscommunication in 1854.

15. The Battle of Waterloo in 1815 ended Napoleon Bonaparte's rule and changed the course of European history.

16. Johannes Gutenberg's invention of the printing press in the 15th century revolutionized the spread of knowledge.

17. Ancient Greeks invented the watermill, which was used for grinding grain and marked a significant technological advancement.

18. Archimedes is famous for his principle of buoyancy and inventive war machines like the Archimedes Screw.

19. The discovery of penicillin by Alexander Fleming in 1928 transformed the treatment of bacterial infections.

20. The steam engine, developed during the Industrial Revolution, powered trains and factories, significantly advancing industry.

21. The Mayan civilization is known for its intricate calendar system and monumental architecture.

22. The Eleusinian Mysteries were ancient Greek religious rites held in honor of Demeter and Persephone, shrouded in secrecy.

23. The Incas built advanced agricultural systems, including terracing and irrigation, to thrive in the Andean region.

24. Ancient Egyptians practiced mummification to preserve bodies for the afterlife, reflecting their complex religious beliefs.

25. The Celts, known for their art and druidic traditions, had a profound influence on later European cultures.

26. Charles Darwin's voyage on the HMS Beagle played a crucial role in developing his theory of evolution.

27. The Silk Road was a network of trade routes connecting China to the Mediterranean, facilitating cultural and economic exchanges for centuries.

28. Marco Polo's travels to Asia, detailed in "The Travels of Marco Polo," introduced Europeans to new cultures and trade opportunities.

29. Ernest Shackleton's Antarctic expedition of 1914-1917 is renowned for its incredible survival story in extreme conditions.

30. The Mayflower's journey in 1620 led to the establishment of one of the first successful English colonies in America.

31. Hypatia of Alexandria, a mathematician and philosopher, made significant contributions to astronomy and mathematics in ancient times.

32. Leonardo da Vinci's notebooks are filled with sketches, ideas for inventions, and observations that reveal his genius.

33. Nikola Tesla demonstrated wireless lighting by illuminating a vacuum tube without physical connections, showcasing his innovative ideas.
34. Florence Nightingale revolutionized nursing with her emphasis on sanitation and hygiene, reducing hospital mortality rates.

35. Julius Caesar's actions contributed to the end of the Roman Republic and the rise of the Roman Empire.

36. The Roanoke Colony, established in 1587, vanished without a trace, leaving only the word "Croatoan" carved into a tree.

37. The Sodder children's disappearance in a 1945 house fire remains a mystery, with theories ranging from abduction to mistaken identity.

38. Flight MH370's disappearance in 2014 remains one of aviation's greatest mysteries, with search efforts spanning several countries.

39. Amelia Earhart's disappearance over the Pacific Ocean in 1937 continues to spark theories and investigations.

40. Jack the Ripper, the infamous London serial killer, remains unidentified despite extensive investigations and numerous suspects.

41. Siberian shamans practiced rituals to communicate with the spirit world, using drums and trance states for guidance and healing.

42. Medieval festivals featured strange customs like jousting tournaments, mock battles, and elaborate feasts with unusual dishes.

43. Hanami is a Japanese tradition celebrating the blooming of cherry blossoms with picnics and festivals under the beautiful trees.

44. The Day of the Dead in Mexico honors deceased loved ones with altars, marigolds, and sugar skulls in a vibrant celebration.

45. The ancient Greek Olympic Games were held every four years in Olympia and featured athletic competitions and religious ceremonies.

46. The Sphinx of Giza, a colossal limestone statue, continues to mystify historians with its purpose and the identity of its builder.

47. The Great Pyramid of Giza, one of the Seven Wonders of the Ancient World, showcases the precision of ancient engineering.

48. The Rosetta Stone, discovered in 1799, was crucial for deciphering Egyptian hieroglyphs and unlocking ancient Egyptian writing.

49. The Voynich Manuscript is an undeciphered manuscript with strange illustrations and unknown text, baffling cryptographers.

50. The Tunguska event of 1908 was a massive explosion in Siberia, likely caused by a meteor or comet, flattening trees over a vast area.

51. The Dead Sea Scrolls, found in the 1940s, include ancient Jewish texts that provide insight into the history and religion of the time.

52. The Minoan civilization, known for its advanced art and architecture, mysteriously declined around 1450 BCE.

53. Petra, an ancient city carved into Jordan's cliffs, was a major trading hub rediscovered by Western explorers in the 19th century.

54. The Fountain of Youth, sought by explorers like Ponce de León, symbolizes humanity's quest for eternal youth and vitality.

55. The ancient city of Ur, a major Sumerian city-state, was a center of trade and culture with its well-preserved ziggurat.

56. The Shroud of Turin is believed by some to be Jesus's burial cloth, and its authenticity has been the subject of extensive scientific debate.

57. The Phaistos Disc, a mysterious clay disk from Minoan Crete, features undeciphered symbols that continue to puzzle researchers.

58. The Mayan calendar, known for its complex calculations, predicted the end of an era in 2012, leading to speculation about apocalyptic events.

59. The Golem of Prague, a clay figure brought to life by Rabbi Löw, is a legendary creature said to have protected the Jewish community.

60. The city of Herculaneum was buried by the eruption of Mount Vesuvius in 79 AD, alongside Pompeii, preserving many ancient artifacts.

61. The Great Zimbabwe ruins, built in the 11th century, are the remains of a powerful civilization and the largest ancient structure in Africa.

62. The Antikythera mechanism, an ancient Greek astronomical device, is considered the world's first computer for its complexity and precision.

63. The Maya civilization developed an intricate writing system, using glyphs to record history, astronomy, and mythology.

64. The Dodo bird, native to Mauritius, became extinct in the 17th century due to overhunting and introduced species.

65. The Codex Leicester, a manuscript by Leonardo da Vinci, includes sketches and writings on various scientific and engineering topics.

66. The Hanging Gardens of Babylon, one of the Seven Wonders of the Ancient World, are described as a lush paradise, though their existence remains debated.

67. The Byzantine Empire, which succeeded the Roman Empire, was known for its rich culture and preserved ancient knowledge through the Dark Ages.

68. The Eiffel Tower, built for the 1889 Exposition Universelle, was initially criticized but has become one of the most iconic landmarks in the world.

69. The ancient city of Carthage, a major rival to Rome, was known for its powerful navy and the military genius of Hannibal.

70. The Battle of Gettysburg in 1863 was a turning point in the American Civil War and is remembered for President Abraham Lincoln's Gettysburg Address.

71. The Colossus of Rhodes, a giant statue of the sun god Helios, stood over 100 feet tall and was one of the Seven Wonders of the Ancient World.

72. The Great Fire of London in 1666 destroyed much of the city but led to significant improvements in building regulations and urban planning.

73. The discovery of the Rosetta Stone in Egypt allowed scholars to decipher ancient Egyptian hieroglyphs, unlocking many historical secrets.

74. The Berlin Wall, erected in 1961, divided East and West Berlin until its fall in 1989, symbolizing the end of the Cold War.

75. The ancient Greeks invented the first known steam engine, called the aeolipile, though it was not used for practical purposes at the time.

76. The Giza pyramids were originally covered in smooth, white limestone casing stones that reflected the sun's light, making them shine brightly.

77. The Roman Colosseum could hold up to 80,000 spectators and was used for gladiatorial games, animal hunts, and public spectacles

78. The Inca Empire, with its advanced engineering and agricultural techniques, was the largest empire in pre-Columbian America.

79. The Parthenon in Athens was originally a temple dedicated to the goddess Athena and is a symbol of ancient Greek architecture and democracy.

80. The Silk Road was not a single road but a network of trade routes that facilitated cultural and economic exchanges between East and West.

81. The Terracotta Army, buried with China's first emperor Qin Shi Huang, consists of over 8,000 life-sized clay soldiers and horses.

82. The Gutenberg Bible, printed in the 1450s, was the first major book produced using movable type printing technology.

83. The Elgin Marbles, originally part of the Parthenon, are a collection of classical Greek marble sculptures that are now housed in the British Museum.

84. The ancient Sumerians developed one of the earliest writing systems known as cuneiform, using wedge-shaped marks on clay tablets.

85. The Rosetta Stone was key in deciphering Egyptian hieroglyphs because it contained the same text written in Greek, Demotic, and hieroglyphs.

86. The Viking Longships were technologically advanced for their time, allowing Vikings to travel long distances across the seas and rivers.

87. The Pyramids of Giza were originally covered in polished white limestone that made them shine brightly in the sunlight.

88. The ancient city of Pompeii was buried under volcanic ash from Mount Vesuvius in 79 AD, preserving it in remarkable detail.

89. The Mayan civilization developed an advanced understanding of astronomy and created one of the most accurate ancient calendars.

90. The ancient Egyptians used a variety of tools and techniques to build the pyramids, including ramps, levers, and manpower.

91. The Great Pyramid of Giza was the tallest man-made structure in the world for over 3,800 years until the completion of the Lincoln Cathedral in England.

92. The Alhambra in Spain, a stunning example of
Moorish architecture, was originally a fortress
before being transformed into a palace.

93. The Mona Lisa, painted by Leonardo da Vinci,
is one of the most famous and enigmatic portraits in
art history.

94. The Hagia Sophia in Istanbul was originally a
cathedral, later a mosque, and is now a museum,
reflecting its diverse history.

95. The Dead Sea is one of the saltiest bodies of
water on Earth, allowing people to float effortlessly
due to its high salt content.

96. The Aztec Empire, centered in present-day
Mexico, had a complex social and political structure
and is known for its impressive architectural
achievements.

97. The Rosetta Stone was discovered in 1799 by
Napoleon's troops during his Egyptian campaign
and was key to deciphering ancient Egyptian
writing.

98. The ancient Greeks were pioneers in
developing early forms of democracy, particularly in
the city-state of Athens.

99. The Pyramid of the Sun in Teotihuacan, Mexico, is one of the largest pyramids in the world and played a central role in the city's ceremonial life.

100. The Code of Hammurabi, one of the oldest deciphered writings of significant length, was created by King Hammurabi of Babylon around 1754 BCE and outlined laws and punishments.

GENERAL FACTS

1. Honey never spoils. Archaeologists have found pots of honey in ancient Egyptian tombs that are over 3,000 years old and still edible.

2. A group of flamingos is called a "flamboyance."

3. The shortest war in history was between Britain and Zanzibar on August 27, 1896. Zanzibar surrendered after just 38 minutes.

4. Bananas are berries, but strawberries are not.

5. An octopus has three hearts and blue blood.

6. The Eiffel Tower can be 15 cm taller during the summer due to the expansion of iron in the heat.

7. Wombat feces are cube-shaped to prevent them from rolling away.
8. The longest recorded flight of a chicken is 13 seconds.

9. The shortest complete sentence in the English language is "I am."

10. There are more stars in the universe than grains of sand on all
the Earth's beaches.

11. The inventor of the Pringles can, Fred Baur, had his ashes buried in one.

12. The original name for Bank of America was "Bank of Italy."

13. A day on Venus is longer than a year on Venus due to its slow rotation and rapid orbit around the Sun.
14. The human nose can detect about 1 trillion different scents.
15. A jiffy is an actual unit of time: 1/100th of a second.

16. The longest word in the English language without a vowel is "rhythms."

17. The Great Wall of China is not visible from space with the naked eye.
18. The human body has about 37.2 trillion cells.

19. A snail can sleep for three years.
20. The only letter that doesn't appear in any U.S. state name is "Q."

21. The longest river in the world is the Nile, not the Amazon as often claimed.
22. Butterflies taste with their feet.

23. An adult human is made up of about 60% water.

24. The Mona Lisa has no eyebrows. It was the fashion in
Renaissance Florence to shave them off.

25. The tongue is the strongest muscle in the human body relative to its size.

26. More than 90% of the world's population lives in the Northern Hemisphere.

27. Elephants are the only animals that can't jump.

28. The world's largest desert is Antarctica.

29. A crocodile cannot stick its tongue out.

30. The average person walks the equivalent of five times around the world in their lifetime.

31. The dot over the letters "i" and "j" is called a "tittle."

32. There are approximately 1.4 billion smartphones in use around the world.

33. A group of crows is called a "murder."

34. The first email was sent by Ray Tomlinson to himself in 1971.

35. The unicorn is Scotland's national animal.

36. A small child could swim through the veins of a blue whale because they are so large.

37. The longest place name in the world is 85 letters long:
"Taumatawhakatangihangakoauauotamateaturipuk akapikimaungahoronukupokaiwhenuakitanatahu.

38. The original title of "The Wizard of Oz" was "The Wonderful Wizard of Oz."

39. The letter "E" is the most commonly used letter in the English language.

40. There are more than 7,000 languages spoken in the world today.

41. The world's deepest lake is Lake Baikal in Siberia.

42. It takes eight minutes and twenty seconds for light to travel from the Sun to the Earth.

43. The human brain is about 75% water.

44. The longest word you can type with just the left hand is "stewardesses."

45. The Great Pyramid of Giza was the tallest man-made structure for over 3,800 years.

46. The dot over the letters "i" and "j" is called a "tittle."
47. There are about 2,000 thunderstorms on Earth every minute.
48. The longest word in the English language with all the letters in alphabetical order is "almost."

49. Pigs are highly intelligent animals and are considered smarter than dogs.

50. The "D" in D-Day stands for "Day," with the term being used to signify the day of a major military operation.

51. The largest snowflake ever recorded was 15 inches wide and 8 inches thick.

52. The longest time between two twins being born is 87 days.

53. The most expensive coffee in the world, Kopi Luwak, is made using beans that have passed through the digestive system of a civet.
54. A bolt of lightning contains enough energy to toast 100,000 slices of bread.

55. The average person will spend six months of their life waiting for red lights to turn green.

56. It takes 21 seconds for blood to travel from the heart to the brain.
57. The first person to reach the South Pole was Roald Amundsen in 1911.

58. There are more possible iterations of a game of chess than there are atoms in the known universe.

59. The human nose can remember 50,000 different scents.

60. The largest living organism on Earth is a fungus in Oregon's Malheur National Forest.
61. The oldest continuously inhabited city in the world is Damascus, Syria.

62. The shortest war in history was between Britain and Zanzibar on August 27, 1896, lasting just 38 minutes.

63. The longest word in the English language is "pneumonoultramicroscopicsilicovolcanoconiosis,"

a lung disease caused by inhaling very fine silica dust.

64. More than half of the world's population has never made or received a phone call.

65. The world's first airplane flight took place on December 17, 1903, by the Wright brothers.

66. The human body has enough iron to make a small nail.

67. The shortest complete sentence in the English language is "I am."

68. There are more stars in the universe than grains of sand on all the beaches on Earth.

69. The deepest part of the ocean is the Mariana Trench, which reaches depths of about 36,000 feet.

70. The largest volcano in the solar system is Olympus Mons on Mars.
71. The only planet that rotates on its side is Uranus.

72. The Amazon rainforest produces more than 20% of the world's oxygen supply.

73. An ostrich's eye is bigger than its brain.

74. An adult human has about 5 liters of blood in their body.

75. The moon is slowly moving away from Earth at a rate of about 3.8 centimeters per year.

76. Honey never spoils, and archaeologists have found pots of honey in ancient Egyptian tombs that are over 3,000 years old.

77. The highest recorded temperature on Earth was 134°F (56.7°C) in Furnace Creek Ranch, Death Valley, California.

78. The first successful vaccine was developed by Edward Jenner in 1796 for smallpox.

79. The Eiffel Tower can be 15 cm taller during the summer due to the expansion of iron in the heat.

80. The word "nerd" was first coined by Dr. Seuss in his 1950 book, "If I Ran the Zoo."

81. The world's largest ocean is the Pacific Ocean.

82. The average person will spend about 6 months of their life waiting for traffic lights to change.

83. The longest-running Broadway show is "The Phantom of the Opera."

84. The longest river in the world is the Nile, not the Amazon.

85. The average human will shed about 40 pounds of skin in their lifetime.

86. The heart of a shrimp is located in its head.

87. The first commercial radio broadcast took place in 1920.

88. The cheetah is the fastest land animal, reaching speeds of up to 60 miles per hour.

89. The total weight of all ants on Earth is roughly equal to the total weight of all humans

90. The Mona Lisa has no eyebrows; it was the fashion in Renaissance Florence to shave them off.

91. The world's largest desert is Antarctica, not the Sahara.

92. The average person will spend about 25 years of their life sleeping.

93. The oldest known living tree is a bristlecone pine named Methuselah, estimated to be over 4,800 years old.

94. The Pacific Ocean is wider than the distance from the East Coast to the West Coast of the United States.

95. The average human brain contains about 86 billion neurons.

96. The most expensive painting ever sold is "Salvator Mundi" by Leonardo da Vinci, which sold for $450 million.

97. The world's largest waterfall by volume is the Inga Falls in the Congo River.
98. The world's largest island is Greenland.

99. The human body has 206 bones, but babies are born with about 270 bones that fuse together as they grow.

100. The human eye can distinguish about 10 million different colors.

www.ingramcontent.com/pod-product-compliance
Lightning Source LLC
Chambersburg PA
CBHW070826250726
48662CB00003B/1097